The BIG Book of Pre-K Learning Centers

Activities, Ideas & Strategies that Meet the Standards, Build Early Concepts, and Prepare Children for Kindergarten

by Diane Ohanesian

New York • Toronto • London • Auckland • Sydney
Mexico City • New Delhi • Hong Kong • Buenos Aires

Teaching *Resources*

To Paul, Erica, and Jordan–
the inspiration for all that I do

Edited by **Immacula A. Rhodes**
Cover and interior design by **Niloufar Safavieh**
Cover illustration by **Peggy Tagel**
Interior illustration by **Maranda Maberry**

ISBN: 0-439-56920-6
Copyright © 2006 by Diane C. Ohanesian
Published by Scholastic Inc.
All rights reserved.
Printed in the U.S.A.

2 3 4 5 6 7 8 9 10   40   14 13 12 11 10 09 08 07 06

CONTENTS

Welcome

Welcome to *The Big Book of Pre-K Learning Centers!* This unique resource is packed with ideas to help guide, inform, and inspire you as you work with the children in your program each day. You'll find suggestions and activities that make experiences in each of your learning centers fascinating and fun, all the while stretching children's minds and imaginations.

My hope is that you will experience this book as an effective teaching partner. Your days are filled with making lesson plans, assessing children's needs, observing behaviors, contacting parents, and much, much more. *The Big Book of Pre-K Learning Centers* is meant to be a hands-on assistant, helping you throughout your day by providing new, innovative activities for each learning center in your classroom.

You'll discover that the most special and unique feature about this book is that it offers a truly integrated curriculum. Each of the five sections of the book is devoted to a different learning center—literacy, math, dramatic play, blocks, and art—and provides effective, creative ways to build a wide range of skills in each of these areas.

Additional activities include ways to integrate seasonal concepts into your learning centers, "On the Spot" celebrations that invite children to celebrate the learning that takes place in each center, and suggestions on using recyclable materials in children's daily center activities.

While we can be purposeful about creating environments, providing materials, and designing curriculum plans to promote learning, how children respond to and interact with these elements determines the different kinds of learning that take place. Use the ideas in *The Big Book of Pre-K Learning Centers* to introduce flexible, cross-curricular activities into your centers—you'll be delightfully surprised by the ongoing, integrated learning that will surely take place!

Diane C. Ohanesian

Using This Book

The Big Book of Pre-K Learning Centers was designed for flexible use. It's a helpful resource to have in the classroom at all times—for those moments when you might need inspiration, fresh activities, or a resource for teaching assistants and families who are looking for exciting, developmentally appropriate activities to introduce to children.

You'll find ideas and activities in this book helpful whether you pick it up at the start of the school year while in the early stages of preparing your learning centers, at mid-year when you might want to re-think and refresh your centers, or at the end of the year to introduce new and different learning activities into your centers.

This book is packed with delightful ideas and projects that integrate almost every aspect of the curriculum into each of these learning centers: literacy, math, dramatic play, blocks, and art. The fresh and engaging activities in each section are designed to help children develop important early childhood skills and concepts while also providing flexibility to address their individual needs and abilities. Here's what you'll find in the pages for each section:

Introduction

This summary provides general information about the center-related activities and experiences found in the pages to follow.

Seasonal Activities

These suggestions serve as a guide to help you incorporate concepts related to each season of the year into your learning center. Spring, summer, winter, or fall, you'll find activities that help children recognize the unique features of each season and take advantage of the different weather conditions, foods, and opportunities that are associated with them.

"On the Spot" Center Celebrations

These activities can be used to interject a dose of "something special" into children's learning during the year. The "On the Spot" celebrations can be used to reinforce specific skills, recognize children's accomplishments, encourage creativity, and provide children with opportunities to celebrate the fun and unique ways they can learn in the different centers.

Recyclable Materials

What can you do with recyclable materials you might find around the school, in your basement, at garage sales, or elsewhere? Check these pages to discover a list of recyclable materials and possible ways to use them in the learning center to integrate and reinforce important skills. Empty and clean the materials as needed.

Activity Pages

The activity featured on each of these pages uses common items found in the center to integrate one or more skills related to math, science, literacy, art (including performing arts and music), or dramatic play. Each activity page includes:

Skills & Concepts – This list identifies skills that can be taught or reinforced with the activity. Of course, learning is not limited to this list—as children engage in the activity, be sure to look for opportunities to teach or emphasize additional skills and concepts.

Materials – Check this section of the page to discover what materials are needed to do the activity with children. Most materials are readily available or easy to gather and prepare.

How To – These easy step-by-step directions tell you how to prepare for and set up the activity, as well as how to engage children in the activity in fun and interesting ways.

Variations – The activities listed here suggest ways to modify, adapt, or expand the featured activity. These ideas can be used in addition to, or instead of, the featured activity, and many use the same materials.

Extending the Activity – Use these ideas to enhance and enrich children's learning experiences.

Connections to the Early Childhood Standards

Language Arts

The activities in this book are designed to support you in meeting the following recommendations and goals for early reading and writing put forth in a joint position statement by the International Reading Association (IRA) and the National Association for the Education of Young Children (NAEYC). These goals describe a continuum for children's development in preschool:

- understands that print carries a message
- engages in reading and writing attempts
- identifies labels and signs in their environment
- identifies some letters and makes some letter-sound matches
- uses known letters or approximations of letters to represent written language

Math

The activities also support the recommendations put forth in a joint position statement by the National Council of Teachers of Mathematics (NCTM) and NAEYC. The statement describes a continuum for children's mathematics knowledge and skills development in grades Pre-K–1:

Number & Operations
- counts a collection of items
- understands "how many"
- "sees" and labels collections with a number
- adds and subtracts nonverbally and using counting-based strategies

Geometry & Spatial Sense
- recognizes and names a variety of shapes
- describes basic attributes of shapes
- uses shapes to create a picture
- describes object locations with spatial words

Measurement
- recognizes and labels measurable attributes of objects
- compares and sorts by attributes
- uses different processes and units for measurement
- makes use of nonstandard and conventional measuring tools

Patterns & Algebra
● notices and copies simple repeating patterns
● notices and discusses patterns in arithmetic

Displaying & Analyzing Data
● sorts objects and counts and compares the groups formed
● organizes and displays data through using simple graphs

Science

The activities also support you in meeting the National Science Education Content Standards. The standards describe which science concepts students in grades K–4 should understand and which skills they should develop. The list below shows how the topics in this book correlate with these standards.

Science as Inquiry
● Science investigations involve asking and answering a question.
● Scientists use different kinds of investigations such as describing and classifying objects, events, and organisms.
● Simple instruments such as magnifiers provide more information than scientists obtain using only their senses.

Physical Science
● The position of an object can be described by locating it relative to another object.
● Objects have many observable properties, such as size and weight, shape and color, and temperature.
● Sound is produced by vibrating objects.

Life Science
● Plants and animals have different structures that serve different functions in growth and survival—for example, humans have body structures for walking, holding, seeing, and talking.
● Humans and other organisms have senses that help them detect internal and external cues.
● Plants and animals have life cycles that are different for different organisms.

Earth & Space Science
● Weather changes from day to day and throughout the seasons.

Sources: *Learning to Read and Write: Developmentally Appropriate Practices for Young Children* © 1998 by International Reading Association and National Association for the Education of Young Children; and *Early Childhood Mathematics: Promoting Good Beginnings* © 2002 by The National Association for the Education of Young Children; *National Science Education Content Standards* published by the National Research Council (National Academy Press, 1996).

Setting Up Your Centers

As you set up your learning centers to encourage integrated learning, it's important to keep in mind that you may need to make adjustments to accommodate children's needs and preferences. You might discover, for example, that larger groups of children want to engage in dramatic play at the same time, requiring the space in your dramatic play center to be expanded. Or you might find that a comfy, pillow-filled space on the floor in your literacy center is more inviting to children who prefer to create stories and drawings in a more private area. As children move in and out of the centers throughout the day, tune in to how they are using the space and materials in order to make appropriate adjustments.

The purpose of *The Big Book of Pre-K Learning Centers* is to provide an integrated curriculum in each learning center. You'll be introducing art activities in the literacy center, math activities in the dramatic play center, music activities in the block center, and so on. In order to accommodate this kind of learning, consider the kinds of materials you provide in each learning center. The following lists offer suggestions for including materials that might not seem typical or traditional for each learning center, but will help expand the ways children use the center, as well as the learning that happens within them. As you browse these lists, pause to consider the many possibilities for using each item to teach skills from other areas of curriculum, as well as the concepts related to that particular center.

Literacy Center
- Teaching clock with movable hands
- Magnets and magnetic items such as paper clips
- Nature objects such as sticks, stones, and acorns
- Envelopes in different sizes, shapes, and colors
- Plastic and foam numbers or number cards
- Lengths of yarn or string
- Play dough
- Dramatic play props such as hats, kitchen utensils, and people figures
- Toy cash register and play money
- Measuring instruments such as a ruler, yardstick, and measuring tape
- Plastic hand lenses

Math Center
- Styrofoam balls in various shapes and sizes
- Pipe cleaners
- Writing supplies such as paper, pencils, markers, and crayons
- Plastic containers in various sizes
- Paint and paintbrushes
- Paper plates
- Supermarket props such as plastic foods and shopping baskets
- Alphabet chart and letter cards
- Plastic or wooden animals and people figures
- Clear shoe storage bag
- Stickers and blank labels

Dramatic Play Center
- Writing materials including paper, pencils, and crayons
- Cardboard for sign-making
- Maps
- Weather-related props such as sun visors, rain boots, and a large plastic shovel
- Outdoor thermometer
- Picture books about life cycles and nature
- Balance scale
- Bedsheets
- Paints and paintbrushes
- Rhythm band instruments
- Cassette or CD player

Block Center
- Picture books about homes, architecture, and families
- Posters of homes and buildings
- Sign- and map-making materials including cardboard, crayons, pencils, and markers
- Index cards and tape or sticky notes
- Postcards
- Chart paper
- Blank booklets
- Plastic hand lenses
- Buckets
- Balance or grocer's scale
- Plastic or foam numbers and letters or number and letter cards

Art Center
- Assorted posters of scenery, people, buildings, and so on
- Picture books featuring a wide range of art styles
- Nature objects such as leaves, twigs, rocks, and pinecones
- Clean, old white bedsheets
- Blocks in assorted shapes, sizes, and textures
- Plastic or foam letters and numbers
- Sentence strips
- Plastic shapes
- Blank stick-on labels
- Plastic animal and people figures
- Ruler and measuring tape

A Word About Integrating Learning in Center Activities

When you think about your math center, materials such as pegboards, beads, pattern blocks, number and shape puzzles, counters, clocks, and measuring instruments most likely come to mind. While these materials are important to have, and to use as math learning devices, it's also important to consider how these same materials can be used to create learning in other curriculum areas.

Let's imagine that children are in the math center working with teddy bear counters. You might witness one child hold up a bear counter to another child and say, "Hello, I'm Teddy. Who are you?" This scenario offers the perfect opportunity to expand learning into other curricular areas! For example, as the children dialogue with their bears, you might ask, "Where do your bears live? What kind of homes do they live in? What do they like to eat? To play?" As children develop the characteristics and lifestyles of their bears, you can encourage them to use the bears to role-play imaginary experiences. Be sure to write information about the bears on paper so that children can illustrate the pages. Then invite them to display their pages in the math center for additional inspiration. By guiding children to explore other areas of the curriculum (in this case, dramatic play and literacy) during a math center activity, you'll be expanding their thinking, as well as their understanding of how learning in different disciplines is connected.

Once you consider the many ways to connect activities in each center to other curricular areas, it won't be hard to see how dominoes can be used as pathways to make-believe homes, how pegboards can be used to create interesting works of art, or how plastic links and linking cubes can become dress-up accessories for dramatic play. When you apply this kind of open-minded planning to the activities in all of your learning centers, you'll discover that the name or nature of a center doesn't restrict the kind of learning that happens there.

■ ■ ■

More About Your Learning Centers

Arranging Your Centers

How you display and arrange materials in your learning centers will determine much about the way the materials are used. Use this checklist as a guide to determine the "child friendliness" of your centers:

✱ Are all materials in good condition and attractively displayed?

✱ Are materials placed in clearly labeled containers and on open shelves so that children can easily make their selections?

✱ Are furnishings arranged in a way to maximize their use and purpose? For example, is a table with chairs available in the math center so that children can work easily and efficiently? Are several easels placed side by side in the art center to allow children to work in pairs and talk as they work? Are private, pillowed areas available in the literacy center so that children have the option of curling up with a book or CD?

✱ Are areas available in each center to display children's work (such as corkboards, open wall space, and hanging clipboards)?

✱ Are there areas in each center where "works in progress" can be stored?

✱ Are there large, open areas (in the block center, for example) that allow children to work freely and without interruption?

✱ Have you taken traffic patterns into account, so that children can freely move in and out of the centers without interfering with each other's activities?

✱ Are learning centers located so that children have easy access to shared equipment? For example, are the art and sand or water play areas placed near a sink? Is the literacy center located close enough to the art center so that paper and writing utensils can be easily shared?

✱ Are children's individual needs taken into account? For example, if you have children in your classroom who are particularly sensitive to sound, you might locate your block center far enough from the literacy center to allow these children access to a calm and quiet area of the room.

■ ■ ■

Storing Materials

Use your imagination when looking for ways to store materials and display children's work in each of your learning centers. Here are some ideas to consider:

Baskets of various shapes and sizes: Use these to store objects such as crayons and markers in the art center; dress-up accessories in the dramatic play center; sticky notes, pencils, and letter stickers in the literacy center; paper for labeling block structures in the block center; and plastic counters and math rods in the math center. Remember to clearly label the baskets, using both words and pictures.

Old backpacks: These make great storage spaces for dress-up clothes in the dramatic play center. You can store items in the backpacks by themes (such as office dress-up, rock-star dress-up, and doctor dress-up), label them, and then fill them with the clothing items and corresponding accessories.

Pizza boxes: Store games and game pieces in these boxes. Make sure you label the boxes with words and pictures so children will be able to "read" the contents of the boxes.

Bubble wrap: Tone down the noise created when children shelve the blocks by taping bubble wrap onto your block storage shelves.

Clothes drying racks: Use these to store and display children's art work in the art center. You can attach the artwork to the racks with clothespins.

Large mailing tubes: Children's artwork can be rolled and stored in these tubes until you're ready to send the work home.

Egg cartons: These make wonderful containers for storing manipulatives in the math center.

Plastic silverware trays: These trays make terrific containers for holding crayons, markers, pipe cleaners, and a number of other kinds of art materials.

Plastic gift boxes with clear lids: Children can place their classroom collections in these boxes, put on the lids, and have an easy-to-view display case.

Floral foam: Press the top end of paintbrushes and markers into the foam for quick-and-easy storage.

Learning With Masking Tape

In addition to traditional materials, you can use commonplace supplies, such as masking tape, to support learning across the curriculum. Try some of these easy masking-tape ideas with children. Then be on the lookout for other inexpensive materials that can be used in diverse and creative ways to expand learning!

Literacy Center: Tape the shape of a letter on a table and have children search for words that contain that letter.

Math Center: Have children match plastic shapes (or numbers) to masking-tape shapes (or numbers) on the floor.

Dramatic Play Center: Tape the shape of a train engine and cars to the floor and invite children to climb aboard!

Block Center: Ask children to estimate, and then test, how many blocks it will take to fill a large masking-tape square on the floor.

Art Center: Let children tape a design or pattern on a large sheet of paper and then paint over it to create an original work of art (the tape will repel the paint).

LITERACY CENTER

Throughout this section, you'll find ideas for introducing science, art, math, and dramatic play experiences into your literacy center. Each activity uses readily available materials to explore not only literacy concepts like letter and word recognition, prewriting skills, rhyming sounds, and left-to-right progression, but also concepts related to science, art, dramatic play, and math. Create messages to put in paper fortune cookies? Move creatively from left to right along wavy lines on the floor? Why not? There are unlimited ways children can use their minds and bodies to reinforce literacy skills, while developing skills in other curriculum areas. So open your literacy center to the possibility of reinforcing skills in curriculum areas from science to dramatic play. Just remember—more than reading and writing can happen in the literacy center!

Literacy for All Seasons

Any time of the year is right for building and reinforcing children's early reading and writing skills.

Autumn Activities

Bring in different autumn-related items such as bright red apples, plump round pumpkins, and crisp orange leaves. Encourage children to examine each item carefully. Then have them describe it, brainstorming as many different descriptive words as possible (*crunchy*, *flaky*, *rough*, *smooth*, *zigzagged*, and so on). Print children's descriptive words on chart paper. Help them use words from the list to create some fabulous fall poetry!

Cut out ten pumpkin shapes from orange construction paper. Print a different word on each of the first five pumpkins. On the other five pumpkins, print words that rhyme with the first five. Help children "read" the words and match the pumpkin pairs by sound.

Have a classroom bake sale. Begin by cooking up some autumn treats with children. You might make pumpkin bread, applesauce cake, or pumpkin muffins. Later, help children create signs and price tags to display with the baked goods. Give children paper money and then invite them to "buy" the baked goods of their choice. Yummy!

Winter Activities

Share picture books with children about different cold-weather activities. Invite them to tell about their favorite wintertime activities. Then give children sheets of white construction paper and crayons to illustrate these activities. Display the drawings throughout the literacy center.

During the winter months, designate one day a week on your calendar as "Warm Up in Winter" day. Use a sticker to highlight that day. When the day arrives, help children follow recipes to make "warm up" treats such as cocoa with marshmallows, s'mores, cinnamon oatmeal, or warm apple cider. As they enjoy their treats, share picture books and poems about warm weather climates and activities.

Spring Activities

Fill large plastic eggs with a pair of plastic letters (use pairs of matching and unmatched letters). Put the eggs in a basket. Then place the egg basket and an empty basket in the literacy center. Invite children to take turns opening an egg and identifying the letters inside. If the letters match, they may pick another egg to open. Have them put the letters in the empty basket. After all the eggs are empty, have children find matching letters in the letter basket.

Visit the library with children to check out books about spring. Back in the classroom, share and discuss important springtime events featured in the books (such as baby animals being born, flowers blooming, and eggs hatching).

For each child, cut out five flower shapes from colored construction paper. Print the child's name on the five flowers. Then mix up the all flowers for a group of children and place them facedown on a table. Have children take turns picking a flower. Help them "read" the name on the flower, and then have them give it to the named child. After children have collected all their flowers, invite them to paste the cutouts on construction paper and add stems to make a colorful spring bouquet.

Summer Activities

Share books that feature summer events such as a trip to the beach, a July 4th celebration, and a camping trip. Then re-create some of these events in the classroom. To reinforce literacy skills, help children make signs, invitations, and tickets to use in the celebrations.

Fill a beach bag with a variety of summer-related items, such as a straw hat, beach ball, and sand pail. Invite one child at a time to remove an item from the bag, name it, and call out a rhyming word.

Turn your literacy center into an imaginary beach! Simply have children lie on towels as they pretend to be relaxing on a sunny beach. Then provide a story prompt, such as "Once a child was lying on a beach surrounded by sand and sun. Suddenly…." Invite a child to complete the sentence. Then have other children add sentences to continue and complete the story. Write their sentences on chart paper. When finished, read the entire story to children.

Display a set of laminated uppercase letters outdoors. Then give children bubble solution and blowers. Have them take turns pointing their blower at a letter, naming it, and then blowing a round of bubbles. As classmates pop the bubbles, encourage them to name words that begin with that letter.

"On the Spot"
Literacy Center Celebrations

Hold a "What Can a Letter Be?" party. To begin, print an uppercase *S* on a large sheet of paper. Have children watch you add lines and designs to the letter to transform it into a fire hose, a snake, or an 8. Then pass out sheets of paper pre-printed with uppercase letters. Invite children to transform their letters into an object of their choice. Later, have children share their creation, challenging the class to identify the letter hiding in the drawing.

Every month, celebrate children's achievements with this idea. Working with children individually, have them fill in the sentence frame "(Child's name) can (accomplishment)!" (For example, "Peter can write his name!") Write their dictated sentences on strips of paper. When finished, invite children to "read" their accomplishments to the class. Display all the slips of paper on the wall along with festive decorations such as streamers and party blowers.

Celebrate the senses with the arrival of each new season! To begin, have children discuss sensory experiences related to that season. For example, in fall they might see trees changing colors, hear the crunch of dry fall leaves, feel the cool smoothness of a pumpkin, smell the scents of Thanksgiving dinner, and taste fresh cranberries. As children share, print their responses on chart paper. Later, display the chart with some season-related items. Invite children to explore the items, using as many senses as possible. Add any new sensory discoveries to the chart.

Host a poetry potluck party. First, display picture books and posters that feature poetry and nursery rhymes. Share some of the rhymes with children. Then pass out construction-paper place mats and a healthy treat, such as corn muffins, fruit salad, or veggies and dip. While children quietly enjoy the snack, encourage them to create their own poems in their minds. As they finish eating, invite children to dictate their poems for you to write on their place mats. After children illustrate their poems, add them to the display.

Recyclable Materials
for the Literacy Center

Include some of these recyclable materials in your literacy center to add interest and surprise to children's reading and writing activities!

Math in the Literacy Center

Materials	Possible Use
Rubber stamps and stamp pads	for labeling and counting
Plastic stirrers	to count and use as "writing" utensils
Twist ties	to count, connect, and shape into different letters
Wrapping paper	for counting, matching, patterning, and labeling designs
Styrofoam trays	to sort and count items beginning with the same letter
Coupon booklets	to "read" and use in money activities
Sales flyers	for recognizing words and using in money activities
Price tags (from purchased items)	for "reading," matching, and using in money activities
Used calendars	for recording events, counting days, and making books
Wallpaper	to count, match, and label designs

Science in the Literacy Center

Materials	Possible Use
Old rubber gloves	for sensory experiences in finger-writing with paint
Sponges (cut into letters)	for exploring absorption while printing letters
Refrigerator magnets	for exploring magnetism and recognizing letters and words
Paper bags	to fill, "label," and use in weight or balance activities
Paint samples	to use as models to create, name, and "label" own paint colors
Bubble wrap	for air and sound explorations and science journal covers
Corrugated cardboard	for exploring textures and making books
Old photo albums	for sorting and classifying items
Three-ring binders	for storing children's drawings of science discoveries
Empty seed packages	to "read" and use in planting activities

Art in the Literacy Center

Materials	Possible Use
Newspapers and sales flyers	to cut out letters to create letter collages
Sponges (cut in letter shapes)	for creating letter and word collages
Paper doilies	to decorate and use as labels around the room
Paper plates	for making books and illustrating words and sentences
Paper towel tubes	for creating and "labeling" unique pieces of art
Catalogues and magazines	for picture reading
Gift tags	to "label" and use with handmade gift wrap
Heavy paper bags	for "labeling" with words and decorating
Cardboard (as in shirt packaging)	for making decorative signs
Vinyl shower curtain	to cut, decorate, and use for making books

Dramatic Play in the Literacy Center

Materials	Possible Use
Plastic forks	for "writing" in pretend food (such as play dough)
Old theater and concert tickets	for role-playing going to a show or special event
Greeting cards	to "deliver" well-wishes, birthday greetings, and so on
Old stationery	for role-playing letter writing
Gift boxes	to hide words and pictures that represent gifts
Luggage labels and airline tickets	for role-playing a visit to the airport
Junk mail and postcards	to use when role-playing a post office theme
Old computer keyboards	to reinforce letter and word recognition
Old telephones and telephone books	for role-playing telephone conversations
Maps, travel brochures, and posters	to use for role-playing travel and transportation themes

And Try This!

Seed Packages Spread out a collection of seed packages on a table. Have children match packages by the seed names or logos on them. After they find as many matches as possible, invite children to show their packages to classmates and tell how they match.

Cereal Boxes Write a letter or word on a sheet of paper. Invite children to search the print on empty cereal boxes to find a matching letter or word.

At the Store

Skills & Concepts

✔ **Estimating**

✔ **Recognizing words**

✔ **Counting money**

Materials

■ Variety of items (stuffed animals, plastic foods, magnets, picture books, and so on)

■ Sticky notes

■ Markers

■ Toy cash register

■ Play money

How To

1 Invite children to name some different stores they have visited. Ask them to tell about things they purchase at the stores. What must they have to make those purchases?

2 Tell children that they will help set up a pretend department store. First, show them the items one at a time. Ask: *About how much do you think this might cost?* Guide them to agree on a reasonable price for the item. Then print the name of the item and its price on a sticky note. Attach the price tag to the item.

3 Have children help arrange the priced items on a large table. Place the cash register at one end of the table. Explain that this is the store.

4 Appoint a cashier to run the cash register. Have the other children take the role of shoppers. After distributing play money to the shoppers, invite them to make their selections and take them to the cash register. (You might limit the number of items each child chooses.) Then have them "read" the item name and price on each tag before paying for their items.

Variations

Remove the price tags from the items. Display the tags and items separately. Help children "read" each price tag and then match it to the corresponding item.

Help children make price tags for toy foods. Invite them to use the foods in a pretend grocery store.

Extending the Activity

● Spread out the price tags on a table. Call out a letter. Then have children find all the tags with a word containing that letter.

● Help children create signs for the different departments in their store, such as "Toys," "Fruits," "Books," and "Check Out."

An "Egg-cellent" Match

Skills & Concepts

✔ **Recognizing numbers**

✔ **Recognizing letters**

✔ **Matching letters**

Materials

■ Three 9- by 12-inch sheets of tagboard

■ Marker

■ Slips of paper

■ 12 plastic eggs

■ Permanent marker

■ Egg carton

How To

1 Divide each sheet of tagboard into four sections. Print a different uppercase letter in each section.

2 Print matching letters on the slips of paper. Then place one slip in each egg.

3 Use a permanent marker to label each egg with a different numeral from 1 through 12. Put the eggs in the egg carton.

4 Display the three letter cards on the table. Then call out a numeral. Have a child find the egg with that numeral, open it, and name the letter on the slip of paper inside. Then ask the child to match that letter to the corresponding letter on a letter card.

5 Invite children to take turns until all the letters have been matched.

Variations

Add a twist by printing lowercase letters, words, or children's names on the tagboard and slips of papers.

Rather than using letters, glue pictures on the tagboard. Label the slip of paper with letters that begin the name of the pictures. Have children identify the letters inside the eggs and match them to the picture that begins with that letter sound.

Extending the Activity

● Put a different letter into each of 26 plastic eggs. Let children open the eggs and then put the letters in order, referring to an alphabet chart if needed.

● Fill each egg with a small object, such as a marble, eraser, or acorn. Have children open the eggs, name the object, and tell what letter the object begins with.

Recipe Magic

Skills & Concepts

✔ Reading
✔ Matching
✔ Counting

Materials

■ Chart paper
■ Five each of a variety of items (crayons, plastic containers, blocks, and so on)
■ Instant camera (optional)
■ Glue
■ Marker
■ Large plastic barrel (or box)
■ Plastic or wooden broom

Variations

Replace the numerals on the chart with colored sticker dots. Have children count the dots to find out how many items to add to their magic mixture.

After children become experienced with mixing the recipe, replace the numerals 1–5 with 6–10.

How To

1 Print a special recipe on chart paper, using the items collected for this activity. Start by listing the numerals 1–5, in any order, on the left side of the chart paper. Then glue a photo of one of the items next to each numeral. (Or draw simple pictures of the items.) Print the name of the item under the photo.

2 Place all the items on a table. Set the barrel (the pot) and "magic" broom nearby.

3 Have a child call out the first numeral on the chart and "read" the item name beside it. Then ask the child to find that number of the item to place in the pot.

4 Have children take turns "reading" the recipe and adding ingredients.

5 After all the ingredients have been added to the pot, invite one child to stir the mixture with the "magic broom." As the child stirs, encourage the others to recite this chant: "Hocus, pocus, what will we see? A pony or a princess, what will it be?" Ask the stirrer to name what imaginary "something" will be made from the magic mixture. Continue until every child has had a turn to stir.

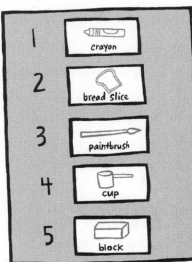

Extending the Activity

● Invite children to draw pictures of the imaginary "something" that their magic mixture made. Bind their drawings into a class book to add to your literacy area.

● Print the numerals and words on index cards. Have children use these and the photos to create and stir up their own recipes.

Cheer Up, Lonely One

Skills & Concepts

✔ **Recognizing numbers**

✔ **Expressing creativity**

✔ **Building social skills**

Materials

■ Plastic numerals 1–9 (or laminated die-cut numerals)

■ Wipe-off marker

■ 9- by 12-inch white construction paper

■ Crayons

How To

1 Talk with children about how it feels to be alone. Ask: *How do you feel when you want to play with someone, but everyone is busy or playing with someone else?*

2 Place the numerals 1–9 on a table. Have a child find the numeral 1 and show it to the group. Then use the wipe-off pen to draw a sad face on the numeral. Explain that 1 is lonely and that children will be making cards to cheer it up.

3 Distribute the sheets of paper and crayons to children. Help them fold their papers in half to make cards. Then have children think about what they want to say to 1. For example, they might say "Dear 1, I'm sorry you are lonely. You can play with me and my friends when we go to the playground." Print each child's dictated message on the inside of his or her card.

4 Invite children to decorate the front of their cards with crayons. Then have them share the cards with the class. Use the messages as a springboard to discuss ways by which children can ask to join an activity, as well as ways to invite others to join their activities.

Variations

Hold up the numeral 1 and have children "read" their cards to it. Then, while pretending to be 1, give a positive, encouraging response to each child's message.

After each card is read, invite children to tell how numeral 1 might respond to the message.

Extending the Activity

● Invite children to dictate messages and create cards for other numerals from 2–9.

● Ask children to draw pictures of themselves inviting a classmate to join their group activities. How many people will be in the group?

Butterfly Rhyme

Skills & Concepts

✔ **Counting**

✔ **Understanding one-to-one correspondence**

✔ **Expressing creativity**

Materials

■ Chart paper

■ Marker

■ 9- by 12-inch colored construction paper

■ Art materials including crayons, glitter, cotton balls, and fabric scraps

■ Scissors

■ Glue

How To

1 Print the poem below on a sheet of chart paper. Display it in the literacy center.

2 Help children cut out large butterfly shapes from colored construction paper. Have them decorate the shapes using their choice of art materials.

3 Collect all the butterflies and spread them out on the floor. Seat ten children around the butterflies. Then assign each child a number from 1–10. Explain that you will read the poem. When a child's number is called, that child—and all the children with numbers that come before that number—will pick up a butterfly and do the action named in the poem. Repeat the activity as often as desired, reassigning children different numbers each time.

I spy one butterfly
Flying in the sky.
I spy two
Landing on a shoe.
I spy three
Sitting on my knee.
I spy four
Crawling on the floor.
I spy five
Going for a dive.

I spy six
Doing silly tricks.
I spy seven
Counting to eleven.
I spy eight
Crying, "Oh, we're late!"
I spy nine
Flying in a line.
I spy ten
Flying once again!

Variations

Try replacing the butterflies with bees, owls, geese, or other flying critters.

Rather than reciting the numbers in the poem, hold up plastic numerals for children to identify.

Extending the Activity

● Show children a plastic numeral from 1–10. Have them count a matching number of butterflies.

● Print a different numeral, from 1–10, on butterfly cutouts. Invite children to decorate the butterflies with the corresponding number of stickers.

Names in the Sand

Skills & Concepts

✔ Predicting volume

✔ Counting

✔ Matching names

Materials

■ Slips of paper

■ Markers

■ Chart paper

■ Sand table

■ Clean, empty plastic containers in various shapes and sizes (butter tubs, tall chip canisters, yogurt cups, and so on) and laundry scoops (all the same size)

How To

1 Ask children to print their name on a slip of paper (or to watch as you print their name). Then have them place their name in a plastic container of their choice.

2 List children's names on a sheet of chart paper. Ask them to predict how many scoops of sand it will take to fill their container. Write children's predictions next to their names.

3 To check their predictions, invite children to fill their containers with sand, using one scoop at a time and counting as they go along. When finished, have them compare the scoop count to their prediction. Do the numbers match? If not, write the actual scoop count next to the prediction and circle it.

4 To continue, mix up the filled containers and pass them to children at random (make sure no child receives the same container he or she filled). Have them empty the container one scoop at a time, counting as they go along. When finished, ask them to find the name slip, locate the matching name on the chart, and then compare their scoop count to the one on the chart.

5 If the scoop counts differ, have the child with the container pair up with the child named on the slip of paper. Ask the two to refill the container and find a scoop count they both agree on.

Variation

Rather than using the sand table, try this activity at the water table.

Extending the Activity

● Print uppercase letters on slips of paper and bury them in a sand table. Have children find the letters that begin their first and last names.

● Have children use scoops of different sizes to fill the containers. Ask: *Which scoop fills the containers more quickly? Which containers require the most scoops? Which need the least?*

Label It—Naturally!

Skills & Concepts

✔ Labeling objects

✔ Observing nature

✔ Comparing

Materials

- Paper bags (one per child)
- Nature items (grass, tree bark, flowers, leaves, and so on)
- Clear 4-pocket photo album pages (one per child)
- Three-ring binder
- Adhesive labels
- Markers

How To

1 Give children paper bags to take on a nature walk. Invite them to collect grass, flowers, weeds, tree bark, and leaves of different shapes and sizes.

2 Back in the classroom, have children place a different nature item in each pocket of a photo album page.

3 To label each item, help children "write" its name on a self-sticking label. Or have them dictate the name for you to write. Have children stick each label to the corresponding pocket.

4 Place the pages in a three-ring binder. Then put the album in your reading area. Encourage children to look through the album from time to time to search for changes in the nature items. Did they find any? If so, discuss why the changes happened. Afterward, you might have children collect fresh samples to compare to the "old" items in the album.

Variation

Fill the album pages with pictures of nature items that can be found in your area. Then ask children to look for items that match the pictures. Have them replace the pictures with the real objects.

Extending the Activity

● Using only adjectives, describe items in the photo album. Ask children to look through the album to try to identify each described item. Later, let children describe the items for classmates to guess.

● Share some nature poetry. Then have children dictate their own nature poems. After children illustrate their verses, bind the pages into a class book.

What Is It Made Of?

Skills & Concepts

✔ Reading object names

✔ Recognizing common materials

✔ Classifying objects

Materials

■ Groups of three or more items, with each group being made of a different material (such as plastic blocks, dishes, and counters, and wood blocks, puzzles, and animals)

■ Instant camera (optional)

■ 9- by 12-inch construction paper

■ Markers

■ Large box

■ Index cards (one per child)

Variation

Place all the pages facedown on a table. Have a child select two pages, "read" the words, and then tell whether the items are made of the same material or not. Finally, have the child remove the two items from the box. Are they made of the same material?

How To

1 Print the name of each item on a separate sheet of paper. Add a photo of the item (or drawing) to each page. Place all the items in a box. Then spread the pages facedown on a table, grouping them by the material that the pictured items are made of.

2 Ask children in a small group to write their name on an index card. Then ask a volunteer to choose one page from two different groups of pages, turn the pages over, and "read" the word for the item on each page.

3 Explain that the two items are made of different materials. Call out the name of the material that one of the items is made of, such as wood, plastic, or paper. Ask children to guess which of the two items is made of that material. Have them place their name card on the page for that item.

4 Invite the volunteer to find the two items in the box. Pass the items around so that children can examine them. Then hold up each item and tell children what material it is made of. Did they correctly guess the item that is made of the named material?

Extending the Activity

Print a list of items for a scavenger hunt. Include items that are made of different kinds of materials, such as plastic letters, wood shapes, or cardboard blocks. Help children "read" the list to learn what items to look for. After the hunt, have children sort the items according to the materials they are made of.

Our Amazing Bodies

Skills & Concepts

✔ **Labeling body parts**

✔ **Recognizing names of body parts**

✔ **Understanding uses of body parts**

Materials

■ 9- by 12-inch sheets of tagboard

■ Markers

■ Clothespins

How To

1 Gather children to talk about all the things their amazing bodies can do. Prompt them to name individual body parts by asking questions such as: *What body parts do you use to climb? To pick up toys? To swim?* Print each named body part on a separate sheet of tagboard to make signs.

2 Invite two children to stand and face the class. Use a clothespin to clip a sign onto each child's shirt. Then call out the word on one of the signs. Have the class point to the sign with that word. Ask the child wearing the sign to demonstrate an action using the named body part.

3 Invite the class to "read" the word on the other sign. Then have that child demonstrate an action using the body part labeled on his or her sign.

4 Repeat the activity until every child has had a chance to demonstrate the use of a body part.

Variations

Invite children to "read" a sign and place it on the corresponding part of a life-size body outline. Then have them demonstrate the use of that body part.

Working with small groups, give children two signs each. Have them "read" their signs and then demonstrate using both body parts at the same time.

Extending the Activity

● Place a few signs faceup on a table. Ask: *Which word has the most letters? The fewest?* Challenge children to figure out which letter appears most often in the signs.

● Label signs with action words, such as *hop*, *run*, and *dig*, and put them in a large bag. Invite children to remove a sign. Then help them "read" the sign and perform the action.

Names in Art

Skills & Concepts

✔ Writing letters

✔ Identifying letters

✔ Expressing creativity

Materials

■ One name card for each child (first name only)

■ 2-inch squares of colored construction paper (20 per child)

■ Markers

■ 12- by 18-inch white construction paper (one sheet per child)

■ Glue

How To

1 Give children their name cards and twenty construction-paper squares. Invite children to "write" one letter from their name on each square, referring to their name cards as needed. They can write the same or a different letter on each square, repeating any letter as often as they desire. (If children are unable to write the letters, have them name the letters for you to write.)

2 Have children glue their letters onto a sheet of construction paper. Encourage them to be as creative as possible by making designs, shapes, or even letter shapes with their squares.

3 Invite children to share their works of art. As they do so, have them identify the different letters in their creations.

Variations

Instead of using name cards, give children word cards. Have them print letters from the words onto their squares.

Let children use letter stamps and different ink colors to stamp letters onto their squares.

Extending the Activity

● Display the works of art on a wall. Have children find the letters of their name in the collages, referring to their name cards as needed.

● Line up children's creations on the floor. Pass out alphabet cards and have children find matching letters in the collages.

Picture Postcards

Skills & Concepts

✔ **Expressing creativity**

✔ **Writing names**

✔ **Recognizing names**

Materials

■ Large box

■ Markers, crayons, and pencils

■ Large, plain index cards printed with "To" and "From" (one per child)

How To

1 Decorate the large box to represent a mailbox. Show the mailbox to children. Ask them to tell about their experiences visiting a post office or mailing cards and letters.

2 Tell children that they will make postcards to mail to each other. Then have them draw a picture on the blank side of an index card. When finished, have them turn the card over and write a classmate's name beside "To" and their own name beside "From" (provide help as needed). Ask children to deposit their postcards in the mailbox.

3 To distribute the mail, invite a child to be the letter carrier. Have the child remove the postcards from the mailbox and pass them out. Help him or her, as needed, to read the names and deliver each postcard to the correct child.

4 As children "read" their postcards, have them identify the name of the sender. Later, you might have children mail a "thank you" to the sender.

Variations

Encourage children to decorate greeting cards to mail to classmates. They can dictate messages for you to write inside the cards.

Have children decorate shoe boxes to make personal mailboxes. Then they can "write" (or draw) messages to mail directly to classmates. Let them "read" their mail at the end of the week.

Extending the Activity

● Bring in a variety of stamps. Encourage children to choose and describe their favorite ones. Then invite them to create their own stamp designs on plain index cards.

● Ask children to dictate letters to their favorite storybook characters. Have them add drawings and then display the letters for all to enjoy.

Super Song Creations

Skills & Concepts

✔ Playing rhythms

✔ Dictating lyrics

✔ Expressing creativity

Materials

■ Rhythm instruments

■ Chart paper

■ Markers

How To

1 Invite children to name their favorite songs. List their responses on chart paper. Then sing a few of the familiar songs with children as they clap out rhythms to the tunes.

2 Pass out rhythm instruments to children. Invite them to choose a song from the list to sing. Have them create and play rhythms with the instruments while singing the song.

3 After performing a few songs together, encourage children to make up new lyrics to one of their favorite tunes. Print the words on chart paper as children dictate them.

4 Read the words to the children's new song to them. Invite them to sing the song, pointing to each word as they sing along. Repeat several times to help children become familiar with singing the new lyrics to the tune. Then invite them to play their instruments to add rhythms to the tune.

Variations

Write the student-created songs on paper. Give children copies of the songs to illustrate. Then have them bind their songs and drawings into songbooks.

Write the words to children's favorite songs on chart paper. As you point to the words for each song, invite children to sing along and play their instruments.

Extending the Activity

● Ask children to describe an interesting item, such as a seashell. Then have them make up a song about the item, using some of their descriptions in the lyrics.

● Hold a lunchtime concert for other classes! To prepare, help children create and send invitations. At the concert, encourage children to perform their new songs for their guests.

Fantastic Fortunes

Skills & Concepts

✔ **Dictating**

✔ **Writing names**

✔ **Recognizing names**

Materials

■ Half-sheet of 9- by 12-inch paper, cut lengthwise (one per child)

■ Markers or crayons

■ Large crescent moon shapes cut from brown construction paper (two per child)

■ Glue

Variations

Prompt children to dictate positive, personal messages about their partners to put in the fortune cookies. For example: "You are a good friend. Good things will come your way."

Rather than messages, help children write the word for a common object. When their partners open the cookies, help them "read" the word to the class.

How To

1 Bring in fortune cookies to share with children. As they break open the cookies, have them pass the fortunes to you. Explain that fortunes are short messages about the future. Then read and discuss some of the fortunes.

2 Tell children that they will make paper fortune cookies to share with a partner. Then divide the class into pairs.

3 Working with children individually, have them dictate a fortune for you to write on a half-sheet of paper. Invite them to add an illustration to the back of their messages. Then have them fold their messages as small as possible.

4 Help children write their partner's name on one brown paper moon. Have them glue that moon to another one along the long curved edge. Help them put their folded messages into the moon "pocket" and then glue the open edges together.

5 After the glue dries, put all the cookies in a large basket. Have one child at a time find the cookie labeled with his or her name. Then invite the child to break it open and read the fortune.

Extending the Activity

● What would children like their fortunes to say? That they will be Olympic athletes? Famous writers? World leaders? List their ideas on chart paper. Later, have them illustrate the fortune of their choice.

● Invite children to make fortune cookies in assorted shapes, such as circles, ovals, and triangles.

What's the Letter?

Skills & Concepts

✔ Comparing

✔ Recognizing letters

✔ Identifying letters

Materials

■ Magazines

■ Scissors

■ 9- by 12-inch sheets of tagboard (one per child)

■ Glue

How To

1 Invite children to page through magazines to find words printed in different sizes and fonts. As they work, encourage them to point out similarities and differences in the words they find. Then have them cut out words that begin with letters they recognize. Help them as needed to cut loosely around each word so that all the letters remain whole and intact.

2 Give children a sheet of tagboard. Have them glue their word cutouts onto the tagboard to create a collage.

3 Have children share their collages with the group. Challenge them to name as many of the letters in the words as possible.

4 Later, invite children to exchange collages with a partner. Ask them to name letters on their partner's collage.

Variations

Invite children to create letter collages to share with the class.

Label each of 26 sheets of tagboard with a different letter. Children can search magazines to find words beginning with each letter, cut them out, and glue them on the tagboard with the corresponding letter.

Extending the Activity

● To help children recognize words in isolation, list a few words from their collages on chart paper. Then ask them to sound out the beginning letter of each word and try to read it.

● Use the collages in a letter hunt! Simply hold up a plastic letter. Then have children search their collage for the matching letter. How many times does it appear in their collage?

Read It on Main Street

Skills & Concepts

✔ **Expressing creativity**

✔ **Labeling**

✔ **Role-playing**

Materials

- Large sign labeled "Main Street"
- Assortment of large boxes
- Poster paints
- Paintbrushes
- Scissors
- Sign-making materials (poster boards, markers, crayons, and so on)
- Tape

Variations

Instead of Main Street, set up a street fair. Help children make booths and signs for activities that might be found at the fair, such as "Popcorn," "Bead Stringing," and "Face Painting."

Arrange the store signs on a table and add picture clues to each one. Have children match each sign to its shop on Main Street.

How To

1 Show children the "Main Street" sign. Discuss what kinds of places and things they might find on Main Street. Encourage them to describe the sights they have experienced while visiting Main Street in their own or other towns. Why do they think the street is named "Main Street?"

2 Explain that children will help create a Main Street right in the classroom! Invite them to paint boxes to represent different stores and businesses that might be found on Main Street. Encourage them to include display windows that show merchandise from the store.

3 After making the stores, help children create signs for them. Guide them to come up with store names that make it clear what kinds of things are sold inside (for example, "Sally's Shoe Store," "Mel's Sandwich Shop," and "Bob's Bike Repair"). Have them tape the signs to the stores.

4 Help children arrange the buildings to create a Main Street. Station children with each building and have them take the role of storekeeper. Have other students role-play shoppers who pass by and window-shop.

Extending the Activity

● Ask children to set up merchandise and a cash register to create a pretend store. Help them make and add in-store signs. Then invite them to role-play salespeople and customers.

● Display the signs on a tabletop. Ask children to find specific letters in the signs. Can they find all the letters of their names in the signs?

Reading Emotions

Skills & Concepts

✔ Exploring emotions

✔ Recognizing emotion words

✔ Expressing emotions

Materials

■ Index cards

■ Markers

How To

1 Talk with children about these four emotions: happy, sad, surprised, and angry. Encourage them to tell about times when they might have experienced these emotions.

2 Print "happy," "sad," "surprised," and "angry" on separate index cards. To help children "read" each word, draw a face that represents the emotion beside the word. Make three or four sets of these cards.

3 Shuffle all the cards and place the stack facedown. Invite children to take turns picking the top card, reading it silently, and then demonstrating the emotion to classmates. (If needed, help each child read the card and develop a demonstration of the emotion.) Have students try to guess the emotion.

4 Broaden the activity by discussing other emotions (such as excitement, fear, and pride). Add cards for these emotions and repeat the activity.

happy   sad   surprised   angry

Variations

After the demonstrated emotion is guessed, have the child describe something that causes him or her to experience that emotion.

Print each emotion word on a separate poster board and add a picture to represent the emotion. Invite children to cut out magazine pictures that represent each emotion. Have them glue each picture to the corresponding poster.

Extending the Activity

● Label index cards with activities, such as playing ball, sweeping, and reading. Help children read one card at a time. Invite them to act out the activity and then tell what emotion they experience while doing the activity.

● Draw a face representing each emotion on a separate envelope. Print each emotion word on a separate index card. Spread the cards out on a table. Then help children read each word card and match it to the correct envelope.

Moving Left to Right

Skills & Concepts

✔ Developing left-to-right progression

✔ Following directions

✔ Expressing creativity

Materials

■ Lengths of craft paper (or bulletin board paper)

■ Masking tape

■ Colored chalk

How To

1 Tape a length of craft paper to the floor. Invite children to draw lines, from left to right, across the paper. Encourage them to be creative as they draw, making wavy, zigzag, or dotted lines, or any other interesting kinds of lines they can think of. Make sure the lines do not overlap each other.

2 Invite children to take turns walking along the line of their choice, starting at the left side of the paper and moving to the right. Explain that the left-to-right movement represents the same movement their eyes make when they read.

3 After walking a few lines, invite children to demonstrate creative ways to move along the lines. For example, they might hop along a dotted line, or alternate stooping and standing tall as they move along a wavy line. Or they might pretend to be an animal, such as a kangaroo or a monkey.

Variations

Help children tape large paper squares in a pattern on the floor. Have them creatively walk on the pattern from left to right.

Tape a long rectangle shape to the floor. Have children move from the left to the right side of the shape while performing an action such as hopping or crawling.

Extending the Activity

● Gather sets of small play items, such as spoons, cups, and blocks. Invite children to create a repeating pattern with the items by sequencing them from left to right as they work.

● Write on chart paper children's dictation about an interesting picture. As you read each sentence aloud, have a child draw a line, from left to right, under the sentence.

37

A Rhyme for Any Time

Skills & Concepts

✔ Rhyming

✔ Following rhythms

✔ Reciting rhythms

Materials

■ Rhythm instruments

■ Chart paper

■ Markers

I see Marie kneeling on one knee!

How To

1 Work with children individually to make up simple action rhymes that include their names, such as "I see Marie kneeling on one knee!" or "Jared is sitting with his eyes closed and has one finger on his nose!"

2 Print the rhymes on chart paper. Then read each one to children, emphasizing the meter—or beat—of the rhyme. Point to the words as you read. Recite the rhyme again, this time inviting children to keep the beat as they say the words with you.

3 Pass out rhythm instruments to children. Tell them that they will use the instruments to play a rhythm to the beat of each rhyme. Then recite each rhyme a few more times to help children become familiar with the rhythm.

4 Tell children that they will now say and play the rhythm to all the rhymes on the chart, except the rhyme that has their name. When the class reaches this rhyme, the named child will put down his or her instrument and perform the action in the rhyme. As children recite the rhymes, have them pause briefly between each one to switch instruments with classmates.

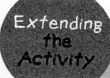

Variations

Invite children to dictate rhymes for you to write on chart paper. Then read each rhyme aloud and have children dramatize it.

List action words such as *jump, hop,* and *skip.* Help children read each word, perform the action, and then brainstorm words that rhyme with the word.

Extending the Activity

● Invite children to add interest and drama by using props to perform their action rhymes.

● Share familiar nursery rhymes with children. Invite volunteers to act out the rhymes for the class.

● Print simple rhymes on chart paper, leaving out the final rhyming word. Have children say the word to complete each rhyme.

Lively Letter Hunt

Skills & Concepts

✔ Following directions

✔ Reading

✔ Identifying letters

Materials

■ Plastic uppercase letters

■ Large, plain index cards

■ Markers

How To

1 While children are away, hide the letters around the classroom or an outdoor play space.

2 Make a clue card for each letter. To do this, draw a simple picture of each hiding place (such as a chair, table, or swing set) on an index card. Also, print the word for the pictured item.

3 Explain to children that all the uppercase letters have escaped and gone to hide! Tell them that they will take the role of seekers and will try to find the missing letters. Hold up a letter to demonstrate what they will be looking for. Then tell them that they will use clue cards to help them find the letters.

4 Distribute the clue cards to children. Before going on the hunt, help them identify the word (and picture) on their card. Then take children to the hunting area.

5 After children find all the letters, invite them to "read" their clue cards to the group. Then have them identify the letters they found.

Variations

After identifying their letter, have children name a few words that begin with that letter.

Rather than using clue cards, encourage children to listen carefully to verbal clues to help them find the letters.

Extending the Activity

● Spread out the letters on a table. Have children pick the letters that belong in their first names. Can they arrange the letters to spell their names?

● Let children create words with the letters. Encourage them to search the classroom for printed words to spell.

Pencil, Paintbrush, or Paper?

Skills & Concepts

✔ Exploring objects

✔ Developing a plan

✔ Expressing creativity

Materials

■ Assortment of writing utensils (crayons, markers, paintbrushes, and so on)

■ Paper in various shapes and sizes

■ Picture books

How To

1 Encourage children to explore and manipulate the different materials in the literacy center. Can they fold, roll, and crumple paper? Scribble and draw zigzag lines with markers and crayons? Make wide sweeps with the paintbrushes? Fan the book pages to create a breeze?

2 Ask children to share some of their discoveries. What kind of things can they do with paper, pencils, paintbrushes, rubber stamps, and other materials in the center?

3 After discussing, have children choose one of the items they explored. Tell them that they will pretend to be that item.

4 Have children imagine that someone is using their item of choice in a particular way (such as folding a sheet of paper in half). How will they move and behave as the item ? (For folded paper, children might bend at the waist and touch their nose to their knees.) As children develop their plans, tell them to keep their thoughts a secret for now!

5 Invite children to take turns acting out the movements of their items. As they do so, encourage classmates to try to guess what item the child is representing and how that item is being used or handled.

Variations

Introduce unfamiliar items, such as oil pastels, a typewriter, and a calligraphy pen. Invite children to explore and then incorporate the items into their role-playing activities.

Have one group page through a picture book. Ask the children to act out an illustration from the book while another group tries to find the illustration being dramatized.

Extending the Activity

Have children create their own picture books or personalized stationery using materials in the center. As they work, encourage children to think about how they move and manipulate the different materials that they use.

MATH CENTER

Throughout this section, you'll find ideas for introducing science, art, dramatic play, and literacy-building experiences in your math center. Each activity uses the existing materials in your math center to explore not only math concepts such as counting, number recognition, patterning, and one-to-one correspondence, but also concepts related to science, art, dramatic play, and literacy. Use pegboards for an exciting art experience? Wood beads and blocks to investigate sound? "Talking" shapes to reinforce literacy concepts? Why not? The ways to use math materials to extend learning into other curriculum areas are limitless! When you open your math center to the possibility of reinforcing skills from science to literacy, you'll discover that more than math can happen in the math center!

Math for All Seasons

Whether it's hot, warm, windy, or freezin', math activities are always "in season"!

Autumn Activities

Bring in a bag of juicy, tasty apples. Show children an apple slicer. Have them count the sections as you point to each one. How many sections did they count? Next, use the slicer to cut the apples. How many slices are cut from each apple? To reinforce one-to-one correspondence, place each apple slice next to a section on the slicer.

Cut out 15 pumpkins from orange construction paper. Draw identical jack-o'-lantern faces on five of the pumpkins. Make two more sets of five jack-o'-lanterns, each set with a different face. Then use the cutouts in a patterning game. Arrange three pumpkins on a long, green, construction-paper vine. Then have a child use the remaining pumpkins to repeat the pattern as many times as possible.

To make a cornucopia, shape and glue a large sheet of brown construction paper into a cone. Fill the cornucopia with real or plastic fruit. Ask: *How many apples are in the cornucopia?* Have children count the apples and report their results. Continue by asking them to count each kind of fruit in the cornucopia. To extend, provide a supply of beads in colors to represent the different fruits in the cornucopia.

Winter Activities

Have children take rulers outdoors on a snowy day. Ask them to find and measure prints in the snow. They might find shoeprints, animal tracks, or prints made by objects that have fallen into the snow. Which print is longest? Shortest? For fun, have children measure the depth of the snow.

Help small groups fold and cut white paper to make snowflakes of various shapes and sizes. Then have children tape the snowflakes in an interesting pattern on a length of bulletin board paper. Have them gently paint over the snowflakes to create prints on the paper. After the paint dries, help children carefully remove the snowflakes. Challenge them to arrange the snowflakes on another sheet of paper so that the design matches their snow-print design.

Snow people come in all shapes and sizes! Provide a collection of paper shapes, including circles, squares, triangles, ovals, rectangles, and diamonds. Invite children to use the shapes to create interesting and unique snow people. Encourage children to share their creations with the class, naming all the different shapes they used. Later, challenge children to use the shapes to replicate their classmates' snow people.

Spring Activities

Cut out bird shapes from construction paper. Write a different numeral on each shape. Then provide a colorful collection of paper feathers. Have children choose a bird cutout, read the numeral, and place that many feathers on it. Encourage each child to ask a classmate to check his or her work. To extend, invite children to sort the feathers by size and color.

Play this version of leapfrog with small groups. Use green chalk to draw lily pads on a sidewalk or paved area. Draw them close enough together so that children can easily jump from one to another. Then write a numeral on each one. To play, name a child and a numeral on a lily pad. Ask the named "frog" to leap onto the corresponding lily pad. Then name another frog and number. Continue play, giving each frog several turns to jump to different lily pads. To end the game, say "Dive!" On this signal, all the frogs will jump off the lily pads and into the "water."

Have children create construction-paper flowers in various sizes and shapes. Then invite them to create an indoor garden on a classroom wall or bulletin board. To make the garden, have children arrange some of their flowers in color patterns, others by size, and still others by shape. When finished, attach a length of paper grass over the bottom of the flower stems.

Summer Activities

Play an estimation game. First, help each child roll and staple a sheet of brown construction paper into an "ice cream cone." Then provide a supply of counting cubes, small wooden spools, or other type of manipulatives. Have children estimate how many items will be needed to fill their cones. Then have them fill their cones, counting each item as they go along. Were their estimates correct?

Use colorful chalk to draw a variety of large shapes on a sidewalk or paved area. Ask children to estimate how many people will be able to fit into each of the shapes. After making their estimates, have as many children as will fit stand in the shape. Is the actual number equal to, more than, or less than their estimates?

What's hiding on the beach? To help children find out, place a large tub of sand in your outdoor play space. Then bury small items in the sand. Invite small groups to dig in the sand to find as many items as possible. How many items did they find? As an alternative, you might ask children to find a specific number of items, such as six seashells. When they find the given amount, they can sit back and relax!

"On the Spot"

Math Center Celebrations

Hold "Number of the Day" celebrations. On a designated day, tell children what number they will celebrate. Then invite them to do a variety of activities that emphasize that number. For example, to celebrate the number 2, they might string two-bead necklaces, make two-shape flowers, create patterns using only two different items, and so on. Also, you might tape a large 2 on the floor and have children march around it two times, or to two rounds of a lively song.

Celebrate "Gumball Days" with this idea. First, locate a clear plastic fishbowl or jug to use as a gumball machine. On each designated day, fill the machine with manipulative items to represent gumballs. You might use plastic shapes, magnetic numbers, animal counters, or wooden beads. Then display a chart with children's names listed on it. As children estimate how many "gumballs" are in the machine, write the estimates next to their names. Then, as a group, count the gumballs and compare the count to children's estimates.

Prepare supplies in advance for spur-of-the-moment mini-parties. Keep a supply of streamers, balloons, individually wrapped snacks, juice boxes, and a "Celebrate" banner. Also assemble a set of paper tableware products for each child. Label each set

with a numeral. For example, write "1" on the plate, cup, and napkin in one set, write "2" on the items of another set, and so on. Then, when an occasion to celebrate arises, such as hosting a special visitor, meeting a class goal, or adding new materials to the math center, hold an on-the-spot celebration. To begin, decorate the math center. Then assign different numbers to children and have them collect the corresponding tableware items. Finally, pass out the snacks and celebrate!

Every other month throughout the year, hold a "growth" celebration. First, write each child's name across the top of a length of bulletin board paper. Display the paper in the math center. Then invite children to measure their height with yarn. To do this, one child lies on the floor while another stretches and cuts a length of yarn equal to that child's height. Then the partners switch places. Help children attach their yarn to the paper under their names. At the next celebration, invite children to compare the new length of yarn that represents their height to the old one. Did they grow? To find out how much, measure each length of yarn with a measuring tape and find the difference between the two measurements. Be sure to describe your calculations so that children can hear math in action.

Recyclable Materials
for the Math Center

Here are some recyclable materials you'll want to have on hand to add interest and surprise to your math center.

Science in the Math Center

Materials	Possible Use
Styrofoam trays	to hold sets of objects for float/sink explorations
Thread spools	to use as units of weight
Bubble wrap	to count and pop bubbles for sensory experiences
Paper towel tubes	to explore simple machines and motion
Small boxes in assorted shapes	to hold mystery items for weight and balance activities
Refrigerator magnets	to explore magnetic attraction of math manipulatives
Plastic containers in various sizes	for measuring and comparing weight of sensory materials
Shoe boxes	for sorting items and pictures by attributes or characteristics
Sponges (cut in numbers and shapes)	for exploring absorption and volume concepts
Aluminum pie plates	to tap out and count rhythms in sound experiments

Literacy in the Math Center

Materials	Possible Use
Newspapers and advertising flyers	to find and count specific letters and words
Postcards	for writing and reading number addresses
Greeting cards	for inspiring number rhymes
Old calendars	for identifying and sequencing days, months, and numbers
Can labels	for "reading" nutrition information and creating recipes
Catalogues and magazines	for recognizing numbers and counting pictures
Cardboard in assorted sizes and shapes	for creating signs and sorting them by size or shape
Paper bags	to label and fill with a specific quantity of items
Plastic berry baskets	to sort and count items that rhyme or begin with the same letter
Twist ties	to count, connect, and form letters and numbers

Art in the Math Center

Materials	Possible Use
Paper cups in assorted sizes	for creating nesting dolls and patterns
Egg cartons	for making critters with specific numbers of body sections
Netted potato bags	to create textured shapes and numbers
Pudding cups	to create repeating patterns with paint prints of both ends
Soap boxes	for making stand-up playing cards labeled with numerals
Empty tape rolls	to make jewelry decorated with specific "gem" counts
Fabric scraps	for exploring patterns, sorting, and making collages
Cardboard pizza rounds	to explore fractions with decorated "pizza slices"
Straws in assorted sizes	for building shapes
Gum stick wrappers	to create shape designs and patterns

Dramatic Play in the Math Center

Materials	Possible Use
Envelopes in assorted sizes and shapes	for sorting, patterning, and writing numbers
Plastic cookie trays	to sort and count play foods
Pasta boxes with clear windows	to estimate and count in a grocery store theme
Wrapping paper	for estimating size needed to wrap "gift shop" items
Plastic soda bottles and lids	to match numerals on lids and bottles and for role-playing
Old, clean socks in assorted colors	to count and pattern sock "doughnuts" and "ice cream scoops"
Plastic forks, spoons, and knives	for one-to-one correspondence in restaurant role-playing
Bottle caps in assorted colors	for coins when role-playing a department store theme
Cone-shaped party hats	to conceal shapes and sets of objects for "magic" tricks
Old date books	for making "appointments" in career role-playing

And Try This!

Jar Lids Collect a supply of jar lids. Tape a construction-paper shape to each lid. (Be sure to use identical shapes on at least two lids.) Then line up three or four lids, each with a different shape. Invite children to duplicate the sequence.

Cassette Tape Cases Cut five index cards in half. Label each card half with a numeral from 1–10. Place each card in a clear plastic cassette case. Then provide children with small manipulative items such as chip counters, buttons, or wooden pegs. Have them fill each cassette case with the number of items corresponding to the numeral in the case.

Let's Take a Look!

Skills & Concepts

✔ Classifying

✔ Creating sets

✔ Counting

Materials

■ Paper bags

■ Nature items (leaves, sticks, rocks, and so on)

■ Textured paper scraps (tissue, corrugated, crumpled paper, and so on)

■ Textured fabric scraps (felt, corduroy, burlap, and so on)

■ Manipulatives with assorted textures (cubes, rubber counters, pom-poms, and so on)

■ Plastic hand lenses

Variations

Invite children to explore the texture of objects around the classroom. Can they find two items with the same texture? Three or more? What texture is most common?

Challenge children to use only touch to explore and group the items into sets.

How To

1 Take children outdoors to collect nature items such as leaves, sticks, and rocks. (Tell them to leave growing plants and flowers undisturbed). Have them put their findings in a paper bag.

2 Back in the classroom, ask children to remove several different kinds of nature items from their bags. Then have them select a few paper scraps, fabric scraps, and manipulatives with different textures.

3 Tell children that they will explore the texture of each item to discover whether it is smooth, rough, soft, hard, or some other texture. Have them look at each item closely with and without a hand lens. What texture does it appear to have? Invite them to feel the items to check their observations. Then have children create sets by grouping all the items with a similar texture together.

4 Invite children to explain why all the items in a set belong together. Then have them count and compare the number of items in each set to discover which texture is most common among the items they chose.

Extending the Activity

● Invite children to examine their objects under a microscope. Have them draw pictures of items with similar textures on the same sheet of paper.

● Play "Texture Detective." First, give children clear plastic dome lids (used to cover sundaes or smoothies). Ask them to imagine the lids are hand lenses. Then have them search the math center to detect different textures.

Float or Sink ... What Do You Think?

Skills & Concepts

✔ Recognizing numbers

✔ Predicting buoyancy

✔ Counting

Materials

■ 10 clear plastic shoe boxes (or similar containers)

■ 11 Pipe cleaners

■ 10 each of assorted waterproof manipulatives (plastic beads, buttons, marbles, rubber shapes, math rods, and so on)

How To

1 Help children shape each of ten pipe cleaners into a different numeral from 0–9. Have them shape an additional pipe cleaner into a 1, so that there are two 1s.

2 Fill each plastic shoe box about two-thirds full of water. Place a different numeral, from 1–9 in each shoe box (the pipe-cleaner numerals will sink to the bottom of the shoe box). Put the extra 1 and 0 in the last shoe box to make the numeral 10.

3 Tell children that you will call out a number and a child's name. That child will find the shoe box with the named number. Then he or she will choose a set of manipulatives, such as the beads, and count out a corresponding number of the items. The child will predict whether the items will sink or float when placed in water. To test his or her prediction, the child will place the items in the water and observe what happens.

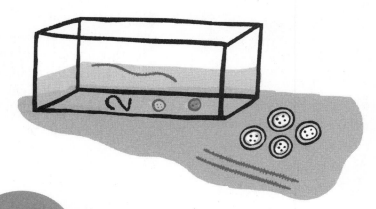

Variations

Try using numerals made of different kinds of waterproof materials, such as plastic or rubber numerals. Do they sink or float when placed in the water?

Instead of using pipe-cleaner numerals, label each of ten index cards with a numeral from 1–10. Attach each card to the outside of a shoe box.

Extending the Activity

● Label one empty egg carton "Floaters" and a second one "Sinkers." As children discover whether an item sinks or floats, have them place the item in the corresponding carton.

● Give children paper bags labeled 1–10. Invite them to collect that number of nature items in their bags. After predicting whether each item will sink or float, have children place the item in water to check their prediction.

Fraction Attraction

Skills & Concepts

✔ Predicting

✔ Counting

✔ Understanding fractions

Materials

■ Magnetic and nonmagnetic items from your math center, including magnetic and rubber numerals, metal and plastic paper clips, cubes, math rods, and wooden pegs

■ Box

■ Large magnet

How To

1 Place all the items in a box. Then have children choose four items from the box and place them on the table. They can choose all the same or different items, or any combination of items they desire.

2 Have children predict which of the selected items might or might not be magnetic. Ask: *How many out of the four items do you think are magnetic (or not magnetic)?*

3 Invite children to test their predictions with a magnet. Were they correct? Help them state their results in a sentence such as "One of the four paper clips is magnetic," or "Three of the four numerals are not magnetic." Explain that children are using fractions! Write the corresponding fraction on paper for them to see.

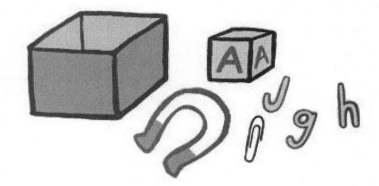

Variations

Have children find additional items from the math center to use in the activity.

Encourage children to predict whether or not sets of identical objects, such as paper clips, are magnetic. Have them try to pick the items up with a magnet. What fraction describes the set?

Extending the Activity

● Ask children to test and sort all the items into two groups: magnetic and nonmagnetic. Help them graph their findings.

● Invite children to test the magnetic attraction of items around the classroom. Have them sort the items into magnetic and nonmagnetic groups. Which is more common in the classroom?

I Like the Sound of That!

Skills & Concepts

✔ **Counting**

✔ **Investigating sound**

✔ **Comparing**

Materials

■ Plastic containers with lids (two per child)

■ Small wooden blocks (or beads)

■ Plastic counters such as chips or animal counters

How To

1 Invite children to count out ten wooden blocks and ten plastic counters.

2 Ask children to place the blocks in one container and the counters in the other. Have them secure the lids on both containers.

3 Have children shake one container to hear the sound it makes. Then have them shake the other container. Ask: *Are the sounds alike or different? In what ways? Which container makes the loudest sound? The highest sound? The lowest sound?*

4 To continue, have children remove five objects from each container, replace the lid, and shake the container again. Is the sound different with fewer items in the container? Have children again compare the sounds made by both containers.

Variations

Encourage children to search the math center for other objects (such as metal paper clips) to use in their containers.

Provide different kinds of containers. You might try chip canisters, cardboard boxes, or sturdy paper bags. Have children compare the sounds made by each container.

Extending the Activity

● Have children add assorted objects to their containers. They might add Styrofoam peanuts, cotton balls, or metal nuts. Encourage them to predict how the new items will affect the sound.

● Ask pairs of children to fill two containers with 2–10 items each. Have one child clap out a rhythm. Then have his or her partner repeat the rhythm by shaking each container.

On a Roll With Gravity!

Skills & Concepts

✔ **Identifying numbers**

✔ **Counting**

✔ **Exploring gravity**

Materials

■ Paper towel tube (one per student pair)

■ Hole punch

■ Pipe cleaners (two per student pair)

■ 10 index cards

■ Markers

■ Large plastic bucket

■ Small counters such as beads, buttons, or marbles

How To

1 Working in pairs, have the partners punch a hole near each end of a paper towel tube. Help them thread a pipe cleaner through each hole and twist the ends together, creating a handle at each end of the tube. Tell children they will use the tube to explore gravity.

2 Label each of ten index cards with a numeral from 1–10. Place one card faceup in the bottom of the bucket. Have children read the numeral and count out that many counters.

3 Ask: *What happens when you drop an item?* After children respond, explain that gravity makes the object fall to the ground. Then have each partner hold one side of the handled tube so that it hangs level above the bucket. Have them put their counters in the tube. What happens?

4 Have children tilt the tube, keeping the ends over the bucket. What happens to the counters when the tube is tilted? Explain that gravity pulls the counters down the tube until they slide out and fall into the bucket. Have children count the items in the bucket to make sure the number of items equals the numeral on the card.

Variations

Provide larger items, such as small blocks, for children to count and put in the tube. Does size change the way gravity works? Have children explain their answers.

Have children experiment with tilting the tube fast and slow. Does speed affect how gravity works? If so, how?

Extending the Activity

● Challenge children to drop items from the tube into smaller containers such as butter tubs or plastic cups. (Attach the numeral card to the outside of these containers.)

● Invite children to use other items such as pom-poms, cotton balls, and paper shapes to explore how gravity works on lightweight items.

Time to Weigh In!

Skills & Concepts

✔ Exploring balance

✔ Counting

✔ Creating equations

Materials

■ Balance (platform or pan style)

■ Assorted items to weigh (wooden pegs, bear counters, math rods, clothespins, and so on)

■ Chart paper

■ Markers

Variations

Cut out pictures from school supply catalogs. Help children write "incomplete" equations using the pictures and then use the actual items to balance and complete and the equations.

Have children predict how many of each item will be needed to balance the scale. Have them test their predictions.

How To

1 Explain to children that they will create equations by balancing items on a scale. Draw two rectangular boxes on chart paper, placing an equal sign between them. Draw a simple balance under the boxes.

2 Write a numeral from 1–10 in the left box. Have a child choose an item. Draw a picture of the item next to the numeral.

3 Have a second child choose a different item. Draw that item in the right box, leaving room to add a numeral to the left of the picture. Read the incomplete "equation" aloud, pointing to each part as you read. For example "Five bears equal (how many) clothespins."

4 Ask children to count the items shown in the left box (five bear counters) and place them on the balance. Then have them balance the scale with the items shown in the right box (clothespins). Have children count how many items were used to balance the scale. Print that number in the box beside the picture of the item. Then have children read the completed equation together.

5 Help children create, "read," and work out other incomplete equations using different items.

Extending the Activity Ask children to count the letters in their names. Instruct them to count out that number of identical items to place on the balance. Then have them balance the scale with a different set of items. Which side of the balance has the greater number of items?

The Name of the Game

Skills & Concepts

✔ Counting

✔ Forming numerals

✔ Sequencing letters in names

Materials

■ Plain index cards (one per child)

■ Markers

■ Large wooden beads

■ 30-inch length of yarn or bead string (one per child)

■ Masking tape

■ Colored dot stickers

How To

1 Print each child's name on a separate index card (or have the child write his or her name on the card). Have children count the letters in their name. Help them write that numeral on the card.

2 Ask children to count out the same number of the dot stickers and wood beads as the letters in their name. Help them say each letter of their name as you write the letter on a sticker. Then have them stick a dot onto each bead.

3 Give each child a length of string (if needed, tape the ends to stiffen them for bead stringing). Have children string the beads, ordering them so that the letters spell out their name. When finished, help them tie the ends of the string together to create a loose-fitting necklace.

4 Invite children to wear their name necklaces throughout the day. Have them refer to the necklaces whenever they write their names, come across a letter matching one in their name, or hear a word beginning with a letter in their name.

Variations

Substitute letter stickers for the dot stickers. Have children find the letters of their names and stick these onto the beads.

Instead of class beads, use large pasta tubes so that children can take their necklaces home.

Extending the Activity

● Write words other than children's names on the index cards. Invite children to create necklaces for the labeled words.

● Use children's first and last names. Then have children choose two or three bead colors. Encourage them to label and string the beads to create a color pattern.

● Invite children to compare their necklaces to learn which names have the most and fewest letters and which have the greatest number of an individual letter (such as an e).

Shape Talk

Skills & Concepts

✔ Recognizing shapes

✔ Dictating dialogue

✔ Storytelling

Materials

■ Chart paper

■ Markers

Variations

Instead of shapes, have children create a dialogue between the numerals 0–9.

Cut apart the shape dialogues. Then cut each strip in two between *said* and the first set of quotation marks. Have children pair each shape with a different quote. Help them read the new sentence.

How To

1. On the left side of the chart paper, draw a circle, square, triangle, rectangle, diamond, and oval. Print "said" next to each shape.

2. Explain that children will create a dialogue for the shapes. Tell them that a dialogue is a conversation between two or more characters. The words spoken by each character are written in quotation marks. Then show them what quotation marks look like.

3. Describe a setting or situation for the dialogue. For example, it might take place on the beach, on a bus, or at an amusement park. Or the characters might be playing a game, eating lunch, or watching a movie.

4. Ask a child to name the first shape on the paper (the circle). Then have the child pretend he or she is that shape. What might "Circle" say to the other shapes about the imaginary setting or situation? Write the child's dictation in quotation marks on the line beside the circle.

5. Have children take turns naming and dictating dialogue for the remaining shapes. When finished, read the dialogue to children several times. Encourage them to read along each time you read the words inside quotation marks.

Extending the Activity

● Ask children to match plastic or paper shapes to the shapes on the chart paper.

● Have children use large shape cutouts to dramatize the dialogue, adding actions and more dialogue if desired.

● Write the name of each shape on a separate index card. Can children match each word to its shape?

said, "Let's go buy some cotton candy and then ride the roller coaster!"

Mail by Number

Skills & Concepts

✔ **Writing**

✔ **Matching numbers**

✔ **Reading**

Materials

■ Blank index cards

■ Markers

■ White business-sized envelopes

■ Plastic numerals 1–5

■ Stamp pad

■ Large wooden blocks

■ Tagboard

■ Stickers (to represent postage stamps)

How To

1 Invite children to "write" short messages on index cards. They can draw and label a picture, dictate a message for you to write, or write their own message. Have them place their message inside an envelope and tuck the back flap in place.

2 Ask children to stamp an "address" onto their envelope using a plastic numeral and the stamp pad. For postage, they can add a sticker to the top right corner of their envelope.

3 Have children build five large block buildings to create a row of houses. Then help them make five tagboard signs, each labeled with a numeral from 1–5. Instruct them to place a sign in front of each house.

4 Invite one child to be the mail carrier. Ask the others to stand inside (or behind) a block house. Have the mail carrier deliver each letter to the address that matches the numeral on the envelope.

5 After children "read" their mail, have them return the cards to the envelopes. Each time you repeat the activity, invite children to switch roles and houses. Make sure each child gets a turn to be the mail carrier.

Variations

Help children add the number word to each numeral sign. Or help them create signs using only the number words.

Use small wooden cubes for the houses. Help children arrange the miniature houses and numeral signs on a table. Have the mail carrier deliver each letter to the correct address.

Extending the Activity

● Have children use the numerals 5–10 to label the houses and address the envelopes.

● Place a numeral sign in front of each block house to show how many people live there. Have children count out and place that number of classmates in front of the house.

Pizza by the Slice

Skills & Concepts

✔ Dictating

✔ Matching shapes

✔ Reading

Materials

■ Round table

■ Masking tape

■ Poster board

■ Markers

■ Paper shapes: red circles, yellow squares, pink triangles, green rectangles, brown diamonds, and black ovals

■ Length of bulletin board paper

How To

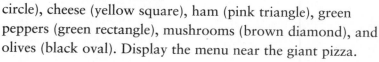

1 To make a giant pizza, tape lines across the table to create six or eight "slices."

2 Make a pizza menu by gluing each kind of shape on the left side of a poster board. Write one of the following ingredients beside each shape: pepperoni (red circle), cheese (yellow square), ham (pink triangle), green peppers (green rectangle), mushrooms (brown diamond), and olives (black oval). Display the menu near the giant pizza.

3 Draw a chart on the bulletin board paper with as many columns as there are children in the group. Write a child's name at the top of each column. Invite children to "order" a slice of pizza by naming their favorite toppings from the menu. Record each child's order in the column under his or her name, drawing the corresponding shape for each topping.

4 Display the chart near the giant pizza. Have each child prepare a slice of the giant pizza with the toppings listed on his or her order. To do this, the child "reads" each ingredient, finds the matching shape, and places a few of them on his or her slice.

5 Have children remove the toppings from their slice. Then have them "read" and fill the pizza order for the child on their right. Repeat until every child has filled an order for each classmate.

Variations

Invite children to prepare two, three, four, or more slices with their listed toppings.

To introduce fractions, have children top half the pizza with one set of toppings and the other half with another set of toppings.

Extending the Activity

● Make an alphabet pizza! Provide a basket of plastic or die-cut letters. Then name letters for children to find and place on their slices.

● Draw a large pizza on chart paper. Add shapes to the pizza to represent different ingredients on the menu. Have children arrange the paper shapes on the giant pizza to match the drawing of the pizza.

What's on the Menu?

Skills & Concepts

✔ Reading

✔ Identifying shapes

✔ Counting

Materials

■ Large plastic mixing bowl

■ Plastic bowls (one per child)

■ Soup ladle (or large spoon)

■ Plastic spoons (one per child)

■ Plastic or paper circles, squares, triangles, and rectangles (five of each)

■ Chart paper

■ Marker

How To

1 Write "Shape Soup" at the top of the chart paper. Then print a simple recipe for making shape soup, drawing the shapes to be used in the recipe. (The recipe might look like the one below.)

2 Display the recipe. Place the bowls, ladle, spoons, and shapes on the table. Then help children read the recipe. Have them work together to mix the "ingredients" in the large bowl, stirring with the ladle.

3 Have children serve the soup in the small bowls. Challenge them to scoop up and name the different shapes in their individual servings.

Variations

Include additional shapes, such as diamonds and ovals, in the recipe.

Tape a large circle on the floor to represent a large bowl. Give each child a shape from the recipe. As you read the recipe, have children jump into the bowl when their shape is named.

Extending the Activity

● Use a permanent marker to draw a different shape on each of four plastic spoons. Have children use the spoons to scoop matching shapes from the bowl.

● Write a letter soup recipe on chart paper. Have children use die-cut letters to prepare the recipe.

● Write a pasta salad recipe. Glue pasta shapes to the recipe (use macaroni, wagon wheels, and bowties). Have children prepare the recipe with pasta shapes.

Stack It Up!

Skills & Concepts

✔ **Expressing creativity**

✔ **Identifying shapes**

✔ **Sequencing by size**

Materials

■ Boxes in assorted sizes and shapes (cereal boxes, jewelry boxes, hat boxes, gift boxes, and so on)

■ Paint

■ Paintbrushes

How To

1 Invite each child to choose a box to paint. Encourage children to paint their boxes as creatively as they desire. They might paint each side a different color. Or they might paint swirls, stripes, dots, or other interesting designs on the box. When finished, have them set the boxes aside to let the paint dry.

2 Place all the boxes on the floor. Have children identify the shapes of the tops of the boxes (such as rectangle, square, and circle). Have them sort the boxes by these shapes.

3 Have children stack all the boxes in each group from largest to smallest, starting with the largest on the bottom.

4 Ask children to count and compare the number of boxes in each stack.

Variations

Rather than stacking the boxes, have children line them up, from largest to smallest, to make a box train.

If boxes are not available, give children shape cutouts of assorted sizes and shapes. Have them sort the cutouts by shape and then sequence them by size.

Extending the Activity

● Hide an item in a box. Stack that box with several others. Then give children clues about the box (such as its position in the stack, its shape, or how it is decorated). After children locate the box, have them guess what mystery item is inside it.

● Ask children to name items around the classroom that are about the same size as a given box. Also have them name items that are smaller, larger, wider, and so on.

● Tape die-cut numerals to the boxes. Name a number for children to find on a box.

Step by Step

Skills & Concepts

✔ **Estimating distance**

✔ **Measuring distance**

✔ **Counting**

Materials

■ 9- by 12-inch construction paper

■ Crayons or markers

■ Scissors

■ Chart paper

■ Paper

Variations

After measuring with individual sets of footprints, have the partners use both sets of footprints to measure the distance. Does the count differ from their individual counts? If so, why?

Invite children to trace, cut out, and decorate their handprints. Have them use handprint lengths to measure the distance between two objects.

How To

1 Have children work in pairs. Ask one child to stand on construction paper. Have the child's partner trace around both of his or her feet. Then have children switch roles.

2 Help children cut out their footprints. Invite them to decorate the cutouts with colors and designs of their choice.

3 Point out two objects in the classroom, such as a door and a bookshelf. Explain that each child will measure the distance between the objects with their footprints. Before measuring, ask each child to estimate how many footprints long the distance is between the two objects. Write his or her estimate on chart paper.

4 Have each child measure the distance using his or her footprints as a measuring tool. To do this, have them "walk" their footprints, toe to heel, between the two objects. As one child measures, ask his or her partner to keep count of the footprint steps by drawing tally marks on paper.

5 Ask the partners to count the tally marks. Record each child's final count next to his or her estimate. Then have the child compare his or her estimate to the actual footprint count. Was the estimate more than, less than, or equal to the actual footprint count?

Extending the Activity

● Ask children to compare the size of their footprints. Which is the shortest footprint? The longest? Have them sequence the footprints by size.

● Put a set of plastic numerals in a box. Have children measure the distance between two objects using their footprints. Then have them find the numerals in the box that represent the footprint count.

Buttons on Board!

Skills & Concepts

✔ **Estimating quantities**

✔ **Counting**

✔ **Comparing quantities**

Materials

■ 4-inch cardboard circle (one per child)

■ Hole punch

■ Buttons, all in one size

■ Chart paper

■ Marker

■ Glue

■ 30-inch lengths of yarn (one per child)

■ Small dot stickers (optional)

Variations

If buttons are not available, provide paper, felt, foam, or wood circles. Or have children use rubber-stamp circles.

Have children estimate how many buttons will cover a cardboard square, triangle, rectangle, or oval. Invite them to glue buttons onto the shape, count the buttons, and compare the results to their estimates.

How To

1 Help children punch a hole near the rim of a cardboard circle. Tell them that they will make button necklaces with the circle.

2 Show children the collection of buttons. Ask them to estimate how many buttons will be needed to cover their circle. Write each child's estimate on chart paper beside his or her name.

3 Invite children to glue buttons onto their circle until it is covered entirely with buttons. (Make sure they do not block the hole in the circle.) They can use button colors of their choice, as well as arrange the buttons in any design or pattern they desire.

4 After the glue dries, help children thread a length of yarn through the hole. Then have them tie the ends together to create a loose-fitting necklace.

5 Have children count the buttons on their circles. To help keep count, children might stick a dot on each button as they count it (they can remove the stickers later). Write each child's button count next to his or her estimate. Ask children to compare the actual button count to their estimate.

Extending the Activity

● Provide a variety of small objects such as stickers, cotton balls, and plastic soda bottle lids. Have children glue on one sticker, two cotton balls, three lids, and so on, to cover their circles.

● Have each child glue only one type of object onto a circle (such as all pom-poms or all wagon wheel pasta). Put each circle in a paper bag. Invite children to identify what each circle is covered with—by touch only!

60

Peg of My Art

Skills & Concepts

✔ **Understanding one-to-one correspondence**

✔ **Counting**

✔ **Expressing creativity**

Materials

■ Pegboard

■ Pegs

■ Colored yarn in assorted lengths

How To

1 Have children count out ten pegs. Show them the pegboard. Ask: *How many holes can you fill with the pegs?* After they respond, have children test their answers by plugging the pegs into the pegboard. Have them count how many holes they fill as they go along. Then ask: *How many holes will seven pegs fill? Nine pegs?* Guide children to understand that one peg fills one hole.

2 After exploring one-to-one correspondence, have children plug ten pegs into the pegboard, arranging them around the edge of the board, in a zigzag pattern, or in any pattern or design they choose.

3 Have children select a length of yarn. Tie a loop in one end of the yarn, making it large enough to slip onto a peg. Then invite children to weave the yarn through and around the pegs on the board in whatever manner they please.

4 To complete their pegboard art, ask children to select and weave several more lengths of yarn through their pegs. Encourage them to share their creations with classmates.

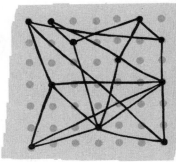

Variations

Let children weave ribbon, textured yarn, or thin cotton cord into their pegboard creations.

Increase the number of pegs for children to use in their pegboards.

Invite children to plug in pegs to create a square, triangle, or diamond. Have them weave yarn in and out, through, and around the shape.

Extending the Activity

● Help children punch ten holes in a tagboard shape. Have them weave yarn in and out of the holes to create interesting designs on the shape.

● Invite children to poke peg "candles" into play-dough cakes. After singing and "blowing" out the candles, have children count and remove them from the cake. Have them exchange cakes with classmates and then count and fill each hole in the new cake with a candle.

What Comes Next?

Skills & Concepts

✔ Sequencing objects

✔ Creating patterns

✔ Following directions

Materials

■ Assorted manipulatives that can be dipped in paint (animal counters, plastic pegs, plastic numerals, and so on)

■ 9- by 12-inch white construction paper

■ Paint

■ Styrofoam or plastic trays

Variations

Have children work in pairs. Ask one child to create a repeating pattern with the items. Have the child's partner duplicate the pattern by making paint prints of the items on paper.

Invite children to use four or five kinds of items to create a repeating pattern. Can they duplicate the pattern on paper using paint prints of the items?

How To

1 Line up three items on the table. For instance, you might use an animal counter, a wooden cube, and a bead.

2 Have children name the items in the order that they are arranged. Then invite one child at a time to repeat the sequence by adding the appropriate items to the line. When finished, children will have created a long, repeating pattern of items.

3 Explain that the items are arranged in a pattern. Have children "read" the pattern by naming each item, in sequence, as you point to it.

4 To create similar patterns on construction paper, invite children to select three of the provided items. Instruct them to dip one item into a tray of paint and then print its shape on the left side of the paper.

5 Ask children to make a print of the second item next to the first print. Then have them print the third item next to the second print. Instruct them to continue making prints in the same manner, working from the left side of the paper to the right, until they have repeated the pattern several times.

Extending the Activity

● Send children on a pattern hunt. Have them search for patterns on displays, book covers, furniture, containers, and other objects around the room.

● Invite children to make fingerprint patterns. They might make fingerprints in a repeating series of colors. Or they might repeat a pattern made up of one fingerprint, then two fingerprints, then three.

Make a Shape!

Skills & Concepts

✔ **Identifying shapes**

✔ **Exploring shapes**

✔ **Expressing creativity**

Materials

■ Large plastic shapes (or laminated die-cut shapes)

■ Large paper bag

How To

1 Hold up each shape for children to name. Then pass the shape from child to child so that they can explore it. Ask questions such as: *Does the shape have sides? How many? Are all the sides the same length? Does it have corners? How many?*

2 Place all the shapes in a paper bag.

3 Have children work in groups of three or four. Ask one child to reach into the bag and pull out a shape. After the group names the shape, have them decide how to create that shape with their bodies. For example, to make a circle, each child might round his or her arms and clasp both hands together overhead. Or all the children might lie head to foot on the floor, curving their bodies to make one large circle.

4 Invite each group to repeat the activity until they have replicated three or more shapes.

Variations

Ask children to form pipe cleaners into simple shapes. Have them replicate each shape with their bodies.

Use tape to create several shapes on the floor. Ask small groups to name each shape and then position their bodies on the taped outline to form the shape.

Extending the Activity

● Invite your "shape detectives" to search the math center for items with a given shape. Ask them to sort the matching shapes by color or size.

● Form two teams for a walking relay. Give a shape to the first child on each team. On a signal, the child finds an item that matches the shape and then passes the shape to the next child. That child walks to find a different item with the same shape. Play continues until the last child on a team finds a matching item. The first team to finish wins!

Cookie Impressions

Skills & Concepts

✔ **Matching shapes**

✔ **Understanding one-to-one correspondence**

✔ **Developing fine motor skills**

Materials

■ Play dough

■ Large plastic plates (one per child)

■ Buttons in assorted shapes and sizes

How To

1 Tell children that they will pretend to be bakers. Give them a plastic plate and play dough. Invite each child to pat out a large play-dough "cookie" onto his or her plate.

2 To decorate their cookies, have children press button "candies" into their patties. They can use buttons in the same shape and size to represent the candies. Or they can use buttons in a variety of shapes and sizes.

3 Help children carefully remove the buttons from their cookies, leaving an impression for each one. Place all the buttons in a box.

4 Ask children to exchange their cookies with classmates (leave the cookies on the plates). Then have them search the box for buttons that are the same shape and size of each impression in the cookie. Have them replace the missing cookie candies by placing each button in the matching impression.

Variations

Have children use an assortment of items for cookie toppings (such as beads, plastic paper clips, and small animal counters).

Invite children to make play-dough pizzas, using an assortment of items to represent toppings. Can they correctly replace all the toppings that have been removed from a classmate's pizza?

Extending the Activity

● Have children use a variety of materials to decorate play-dough birthday cakes. They might edge their cakes with pipe-cleaner icing, add small plastic flowers around the side, and poke peg candles in the top. Encourage them to use their cakes in a pretend birthday party.

● Ask children to place a large play-dough cookie on a metal cookie sheet. Have them attach a magnetic numeral to the cookie sheet and then add that number of toppings to the cookie.

Count on Me!

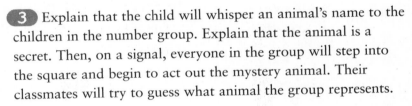
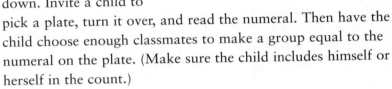

Skills & Concepts

✔ Identifying numbers

✔ Counting

✔ Role-playing animals

Materials

■ 5 paper plates

■ Markers

■ Masking Tape

How To

1 On the floor, tape a square large enough for five children to fit and move around in freely.

2 Print each numeral from 1–5 on a separate paper plate. Spread the plates on a table, printed side down. Invite a child to pick a plate, turn it over, and read the numeral. Then have the child choose enough classmates to make a group equal to the numeral on the plate. (Make sure the child includes himself or herself in the count.)

3 Explain that the child will whisper an animal's name to the children in the number group. Explain that the animal is a secret. Then, on a signal, everyone in the group will step into the square and begin to act out the mystery animal. Their classmates will try to guess what animal the group represents.

4 After the class correctly guesses the animal, ask one animal at a time to step out of the square. Have children count each animal as it leaves the square.

5 Repeat the game, giving each child a turn to pick a numeral plate and name an animal to act out.

Variations

Tape several different shapes on the floor. When a group is formed and ready to act out its animal, name which shape they will step into to do their performance.

Invite children to name things other than animals to act out, such as robots, circus performers, insects, or vehicles.

Extending the Activity

● Distribute the numeral plates to children. Have them line up in order, according to the numerals on their plates. Then invite them to parade their numerals around the square to some lively marching music.

● Provide animal counters. Have children count out the number of animals that corresponds to the numeral on their plate.

Party Time!

Skills & Concepts

✔ **Understanding one-to-one correspondence**

✔ **Counting**

✔ **Role-playing**

Materials

(one per child:)

■ Gift-wrapped shoe boxes (with lids and boxes wrapped separately)

■ Toy prizes

■ Party hats

■ Paper plates

■ Napkins

■ Plastic forks

■ Juice boxes

■ Individually wrapped snacks

How To

1 Put a toy prize in each shoe box. Place the lid on the box.

2 Set the party items—including the shoe boxes—in the middle of the table, making sure the number of each item equals the number of children in the group. Seat children at the table. Tell them that today is special—it's a party day!

3 Ask one child to pass out a party hat to each child. How many hats did the child pass out? Have a second child pass out the plates, another the napkins, and so on, until all the party items have been distributed and counted.

4 Begin the party! Invite children to enjoy their party treats. When finished eating, let them open the gifts to discover what surprises are inside their boxes. Then have them play a counting game and sing some lively counting songs.

Variation

Label each of ten party hats with a numeral from 1–10. Similarly label all the other party items, as well as ten index cards. Give each child a numeral card. Have the child collect all the party items labeled with a matching numeral.

Extending the Activity

● Provide gelatin, cake, or cookie treats in different shapes. Before eating, have children name the shape of their treats.

● After the party, place a mystery item in each gift box (you might use some of the party items as well as items around the room). As you give clues about the mystery item in each box, challenge children to guess its identity.

DRAMATIC PLAY CENTER

I n this section, you'll find ideas for introducing science, art, math, and literacy-building experiences into your dramatic play center. Use these activities to explore science concepts such as animal life cycles and weather, reinforce math concepts such as number recognition and size relationships, inspire creative expression, and encourage emerging literacy concepts. Remember—more than dramatic play can happen in your dramatic play center. Explore the possibilities of reinforcing skills in curriculum areas from science to art.

Dramatic Play for All Seasons

All through the year, each season brings new inspiration for dramatic play activities.

Autumn Activities

Go outdoors with children to collect colorful fall leaves. Back in the classroom, invite children to explore the texture, shape, size, and color of the leaves. Then hold several leaves overhead and let them fall to the ground. Ask children to imagine they are falling leaves. How will they move on a calm day? A windy day? A rainy day? Invite them to act out falling leaves under different kinds of conditions.

Tape a large circle on the floor to represent a large barrel. Ask a small group to imagine that the barrel is full of water. Invite a child to jump into the barrel and then move and bob around like a floating apple. Call the other children, one at a time, to join the first child. Later, invite children to take turns "bobbing" for imaginary apples in the barrel.

Invite children to work together to paint a large fall tree on bulletin board paper. Cut out the tree and display it as a backdrop in the dramatic play area. Encourage children to incorporate the tree in their dramatic play activities. For example, they might role-play an outdoor costume party, an adventure in a magic forest, or a group of busy squirrels preparing for the winter.

Winter Activities

Discuss with children what different animals do when winter weather arrives. You might talk about hibernating bears, migrating geese, food-gathering squirrels, and burrow-digging rabbits. Afterward, ask children to pretend the dramatic play area is a large outdoor area with trees and a lake. Invite them to act out different kinds of animals preparing for the winter.

Add some holiday cheer with this idea. First, invite children to help gift-wrap and decorate an assortment of boxes with ribbon, yarn, lace, bows, and paper tags. Put the "gifts" in the dramatic play center. Encourage children to use them as they role-play holiday celebrations and gift exchanges.

Help children cut out snowflakes from folded sheets of white paper. String some of the snowflakes onto yarn to create garlands. Attach a length of yarn to other snowflakes. Hang the garland and individual snowflakes in your dramatic play center. Then invite children to role-play outdoor wintry activities and sports in your indoor winter wonderland.

Spring Activities

Invite children to spring into action when they role-play growing plants. First, share a few books and pictures that show the growth cycle of plants. After children understand the basic stages, invite them to pretend they are a seed in the ground. Have them pantomime the growth of the seed into an adult plant.

Have children create fabulous flowers using construction paper, paints, crayons, and other craft materials of their choice. Use the flowers to create a flower-garden scene on the walls of the dramatic play area. You might also attach flowers to furniture and other fixtures in the center. Encourage children to visit the garden to "pick" flowers or act out make-believe stories. They might also pretend to be insects or animals in the garden.

What kind of animals hatch from eggs? After sharing their responses, invite children to role-play egg-hatching animals. For each child, cut an egg from a large sheet of white construction paper. Draw a zigzag line across the middle to represent a cracked egg. Then cut an oval flap in the center of the egg. To use, children hold the egg in front of their face. They pretend to be an animal breaking out of its egg. As they emerge, they open the flap and peer through the opening to view their new world. When totally hatched, the animal "sheds" its egg and begins life outside the shell!

Summer Activities

Hold a summer carnival in the dramatic play area! Post a large sign labeled "Great Summer Carnival." Add carnival-related props such as popcorn boxes filled with packing peanuts, inverted party hats containing thinly stretched cotton balls (cotton candy), plastic hot dogs and buns, ticket rolls, prizes, and so on. Tape large construction-paper shapes to the floor. Label each shape with the name of a ride. For example, you might label a circle "Ferris Wheel," a square "Fun House," and a wide curvy shape "Roller Coaster." Invite small groups to visit the center to role-play a day at the carnival.

Set out beach mats or towels, beach chairs, sunglasses, sun visors, beach balls and other beach-related items. Then invite children to head to the beach for some sunny role-playing fun!

Place an empty picnic basket and a blanket in the dramatic play area. Explain that small groups can use the items for a pretend picnic. Invite children to spread out the blanket, take a seat on it, and then unpack the picnic basket. Encourage them to pass out imaginary plates, napkins, and cups; set out imaginary sandwich fixings; and prepare and eat imaginary food. While role-playing, children might even encounter a few imaginary picnic pests, such as ants or bees.

"On the Spot"
Dramatic Play Center Celebrations

Set aside special days throughout the year to celebrate community workers. On the designated day, supply the dramatic play center with dress-up clothes and props related to a variety of community workers. Then invite children to dress up as the community worker of their choice. Have them also gather any props related to their character. After a period of role-playing, ring a bell and tell the community workers that it's break time. Seat them at a table, provide a light snack, and encourage each one to tell about his or her work.

Periodically hold a "This is How I Feel" day. First, cover a table with a length of white bulletin board paper. Have children choose an area of the table to draw on. Then give them crayons and a file folder. Instruct children to stand the folders on the table to create a screen for their drawings. Then have them draw faces that show how they feel on that day. When finished, ask them to lay the folder on top of their drawings. Invite one child at a time to use facial expressions or gestures to demonstrate how he or she feels. After the group guesses how the child feels, ask the child to reveal his or her drawing.

What is today's dramatic play theme? Let children toss a coin to find out! Gather props, dress-up clothes, and other dramatic play items for three or four different themes. Put the items for each theme in a separate storage container. Tape a sheet of construction paper onto the containers, using a different color for each one. Then tape a matching sheet of paper to a poster board. To decide the surprise theme, a child tosses a coin onto a color on the poster board. The group then finds the container marked with the matching color, opens it, and uses the items inside for their dramatic play activities.

In the dramatic play center, any season is in season! Liven up the center by decorating it to represent a season other than the actual season. For example, in the winter you might add summer weather props and decorations (sunglasses, beach towels, a plastic swimming pool "lake," and so on). The switch in seasons is sure to inspire young imaginations and add a little seasoning to children's dramatic play activities!

Recyclable Materials
for the Dramatic Play Center

Here are some recyclable materials you'll want to have on hand to add interest and surprise to your dramatic play area.

Math in the Dramatic Play Center

Materials	Possible Use
Plastic bottle caps	to use as play money
Sticky note pads	for creating price tags for items in store role-playing
Cardboard pizza rounds	to explore fractions with pretend cake or pie slices
Six-pack soda bottle cartons	for sorting sodas, cans, and other items in store play
Belts in assorted sizes	to sort and sequence widths and lengths of car "safety belts"
Expired coupon booklets	for use in role-playing store themes
Plastic jugs and cartons in assorted sizes	to explore volume in cooking themes
Old gift bags	to sort "toy store" items by size
Large buttons and jug lids	to attach to paper strips and use as watches
Rubber stamps and stamp pads	for patterning and counting stamps at the "post office"

Science in the Dramatic Play Center

Materials	Possible Use
Fabric scraps	to explore absorption in housekeeping themes
Netted potato or onion bags	to sort and classify plastic and stuffed animals
Corrugated paper and sandpaper	to explore sounds with pretend instruments
Old backpacks	to carry supplies for "archaeological digs"
Empty spray bottles	for use in role-playing farmers and gardeners
Refrigerator magnets	to explore magnetic properties in housekeeping themes
Empty food boxes and labeled cans	to use in "preparing" nutritious meals
Rubber gloves	for using as garden gloves in gardening themes
Empty liquid-soap pumps	for scrubbing hands when role-playing doctors and dentists
Paper towel tubes	for telescopes and binoculars when role-playing scientists

Literacy in the Dramatic Play Center

Materials	Possible Use
Take-out menus	for restaurant role-playing
Postcards	to picture-read imaginary sightseeing activities
Paper placemats	to decorate and create signs for store and travel themes
Empty pasta boxes with clear windows	for "picture-taking" and describing scenes
Maps	for "reading" during pretend travel activities
Posters	to display in housekeeping area, doctor's office, and so on
Junk mail	to deliver and "read" in post office dramatizations
Old catalogs, magazines, and flyers	to put in waiting areas at airport, dentist's office, and so on
Stationery and pieces of wrapping paper	to "write" letters for post office or travel themes
Large, empty cereal boxes	to sort books for library play

Art in the Dramatic Play Center

Materials	Possible Use
Cardboard boxes with handles	to decorate and use as suitcases when role-playing travelers
Plastic soda can rings	for creating bracelets and belts for fashion shows
Large paper bags	to create and decorate vests for dress-up activities
Chip canisters with lids	to create and decorate shakers for band play
Old photo albums	to fill with art "masterpieces" for art gallery show
Old pillowcases	to decorate and use as aprons for kitchen play
Empty glue-stick tubes	to paint-print "wrapping" paper designs for gift-shop play
Paper cups in assorted sizes	to create animal hand-puppets for farm or zoo dramatizations
Envelopes in assorted sizes	to decorate and use as purses and wallets
Tissue boxes	to decorate and use as jewelry and keepsake boxes

⋯⋯ And Try This! ⋯⋯

Pudding Cups Provide pudding cups and a variety of materials, such as cotton balls, short pieces of yarn, shredded paper, and hole-punch dots. Invite children to fill each cup with one of the materials. Then have them serve the pretend dishes or desserts during an imaginary meal.

Plastic Lids Collect lids of various sizes from plastic cups, canisters, and jars. Have children use permanent markers and paint pens to decorate the lids to represent different food items. For example, they might use cup lids as cookies or pancakes and peanut-butter jar lids as meat patties. Invite children to use the decorated lids in food-related role-playing activities.

Animal Names and Numbers

Skills & Concepts
✔ **Expressing creativity**
✔ **Matching numerals**
✔ **Identifying animals**

Materials
■ Paper plates
(one per child)

■ Markers or crayons

■ Wide craft sticks
(one per child)

■ Glue

■ 10 sheets of tagboard

■ 10 index cards

How To

1 Invite children to share information about their favorite animals. What do the animals look like? What special features or abilities do they have? After discussing, tell children that they will make animal puppets, but will keep the identity of their animals secret.

2 Have children draw the animal of their choice on a paper plate. They might draw the entire creature if the animal is small, or just the head if the animal is large. When finished, help them glue a craft-stick handle to their puppet.

3 Print a different numeral from 1–10 on each sheet of tagboard and each index card. Then tape the tagboard numbers in order on the floor.

4 Give a child a number card. Have the child find and stand on the matching number on the floor. Then ask the child to pantomime the actions and sounds of his or her animal, using the puppet as a prop. Can classmates name the animal?

5 Continue play, giving each child a turn to role-play and perform the actions of his or her animal.

Variations

Invite children to make puppets of their favorite storybook characters and use them to act out a story.

Draw dots instead of numerals on the index cards. Have children match the number of dots on their card to the numeral on the floor.

Extending the Activity

● Print large number signs to hold up. Have children read each numeral and then make their animal's sound or perform an action that many times. For example, they might bark eight times, jump five times, or roar seven times.

● Invite children to decorate paper bags to use as animal costumes. After cutting out arm and neck holes, let children wear their costumes and use their puppets in animal-related role-playing themes.

A Stack of Surprises

Skills & Concepts

✔ **Understanding size relationships**

✔ **Comparing**

✔ **Sequencing**

Materials

■ Cardboard boxes with flaps or lids (in assorted sizes)

■ Variety of dramatic play items in different sizes

How To

1 Collect one box for each child in the group. Select a small dramatic play item (such as a police badge) to put in the smallest box, a slightly larger one to put in the next smallest box, and so on until you fill the largest box with a large item (such as a firefighter's boot). Close all the boxes.

2 Have children stack the boxes by size, starting with the largest on the bottom and ending with the smallest on top.

3 Invite one child at a time to remove the top box, open it, and show classmates the item inside. Ask them to tell what the item might be used for. Continue until all the children have opened a box.

4 Encourage children to use their items to create skits or dramatic play scenarios. Later, invite them to share their "performance" with the class.

Variations

Fill the boxes with items related to the same theme, such as a hospital or restaurant theme.

Instead of boxes, use assorted sizes of another type of container, such as buckets or bags. Have children line up the containers by size, from smallest to largest.

Extending the Activity

● Print a different numeral on each box. Have children take turns finding boxes labeled with a given number. When they locate the specified box, ask them to compare its size to the other boxes. Is it small, medium, or large?

● Have children sequence a variety of items by size. They might sequence cups, chairs, stuffed animals, dress-up shoes, or plastic foods. Ask them to point to the largest and then the smallest items in their sequences.

Take a Number!

Skills & Concepts

✔ **Sorting shapes**

✔ **Matching numbers**

✔ **Following directions**

Materials

■ Assorted paper shapes and colors to represent deli meats and cheeses

■ Styrofoam trays

■ Index cards

■ Markers

■ 10 sheets of tagboard

■ Apron and chef's hat

How To

1 Invite children to talk about their experiences visiting a deli. Explain that customers at a deli order sandwiches and deli workers make the sandwiches.

2 Solicit children's help to set up a deli. Have them sort the colored shapes onto the trays and decide what deli item each shape represents. For example, pink squares might be ham, tan circles turkey, brown ovals roast beef, yellow triangles cheese, and white rectangles bread. Write the name of each item on an index card and attach it to the corresponding tray. Ask children to line up the food trays, with the bread at the beginning of the line.

3 Print a numeral from 1–10 on each sheet of tagboard and on each of ten index cards. Have children stack the tagboard number signs next to the bread and place the number cards nearby.

4 To use, each "customer" takes a number card. Then a "deli worker," wearing an apron and chef's hat, holds up the top number sign. The customer with the matching number card gives his or her order to the deli worker to fill. Continue until every customer has ordered.

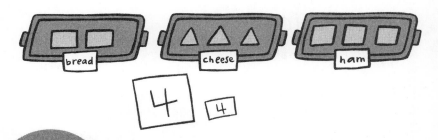

Variations

Replace the printed numeral on each tagboard sign and index card with a corresponding number of rubber-stamp designs. Then have "customers" count the designs to match their cards to the sign displayed by the deli worker.

Set up other kinds of shops in which customers are called by number to be served, such as a bakery or pharmacy.

Extending the Activity

● Provide play money and a cash register. Have the deli worker "ring up" each customer's order. Then have the customer pay with play money.

● To reinforce counting, limit the number of items that customers can order on their sandwiches, not including the two slices of bread in the count.

Dress-up by the Number

Skills & Concepts

✔ Matching numerals

✔ Cooperating

✔ Expressing creativity

Materials

■ Pocket chart (or shoe storage bag with clear pockets)

■ Index cards

■ Plain stick-on name tags

■ Markers

■ Dress-up clothes and dramatic play items

How To

1 Determine how many index cards can be displayed in the pocket chart. Then print a numeral from 1–10 on that number of index cards. You can prepare more than one card for each number. Label an identical set of name tags.

2 Place the number cards facedown in the pocket chart. Display the pocket chart in the dramatic play center.

3 Stick each name tag onto an article of dress-up clothing or a dramatic play item in the center.

4 Invite each child to choose a card from the pocket chart. Have the child read the numeral and then find an item marked with the same numeral. Have children take several turns until each one has three or four dress-up items.

5 Encourage children to work together to plan and perform a skit using the items they selected.

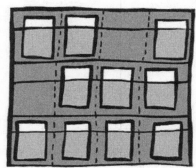

Variations

Print only numerals 1–5 on the cards, and do not prepare the name tag numbers. To use, have children pick a card and select that many items to use in their skit.

Instead of numerals, place dot stickers on the cards. Have children count the dots and find an item labeled with the corresponding numeral.

Extending the Activity

● Hide the number cards around the center. Assign children a number from 1–10 and have them search for cards with that number. When they find one, have them use an item in that area of the center.

● Invite children to put together costumes from the dramatic play area. Then have them select a card from the chart. After they read the numeral, ask children to perform that many actions related to their dress-up character.

Weigh and Play

Math

Skills & Concepts

✔ Predicting

✔ Comparing weights

✔ Expressing creativity

Materials

◼ Balance

◼ Large box

◼ Items small enough to place on a balance and related to a specific play theme (zoo, doctor, restaurant, and so on)

How To

1 Put the collection of items in the box. Make sure the items relate to a specific play theme. For example, for a zoo theme, you might fill the box with stuffed, plastic, and puppet animals, grooming brushes, feeding dishes, and so on.

2 Tell children the dramatic play theme (zoo). Explain that each child can choose two items from the box that he or she would like to use in play. But the child may take only one item at a time into the dramatic play center.

3 To determine which item the child will use, have him or her predict which of the two items weighs less. Then have the child place the items on a balance. Which one weighs less? Let the child take that item into the center.

4 Invite children to return to the box to select other pairs of items. Each time, have them weigh the items to find out which one weighs less.

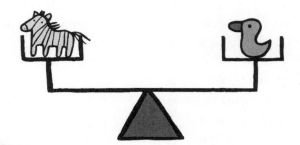

Variations

Ask children to choose two items that might weigh the same. If the items balance the scale, they take both into the center. If not, they take in the item that weighs less.

Put each item into a separate paper bag. Invite each child to pick two bags, weigh them, and open the bag that weighs less. Invite the child to use that item in the center.

Extending the Activity

● Have children sort items from the box. (They might sort the zoo-related items by plastic animals, stuffed animals, clothes, animal-care items, and so on.) Then have them choose two items from the same category to weigh and compare.

● Introduce a variety of scales, such as a bathroom scale, a balance, and a grocer's scale, for children to use in role-playing. For a zoo theme, they might balance buckets of "food" or compare the weights of different-sized animals.

Growing, Growing... Grown!

Skills & Concepts

✔ Matching animal names

✔ Sequencing

✔ Understanding life cycles

Materials

■ Picture books that feature life cycles of animals (butterflies, frogs, chicks, grass-hoppers, and so on)

■ Index cards

■ Markers

How To

1 Encourage children to explore the books to learn about the life cycle of animals such as butterflies, frogs, chicks, and grasshoppers. Invite them to share their discoveries with classmates.

2 Ask each child to choose one of the animals discussed. Print the name of the child's animal choice on an index card and give the card to the child. Then print a master set of cards that contains one card for each kind of animal selected by children. Add a simple drawing of the animal to each card in the master set.

3 Hold up a card from the master set. Ask children to "read" the card and then check the animal name on their card to see if it matches the one on the master card.

4 Have each child who has a matching card act out the life cycle of the named animal, starting at the earliest stage (such as hatching from an egg) and growing into the adult animal (a chicken that lays eggs). Repeat until every child has acted out the life cycle of an animal.

Variations

Have children work in pairs. Ask one child to narrate the life cycle of the animal while the other child acts it out. Then have them switch roles.

After discussing animal life cycles, write the name of each animal on a separate card. Give each child an animal card. Help the child read the card. Then have him or her act out the animal's life cycle.

Extending the Activity

● As children act out their animal life cycles, invite them to use props such as boxes (eggs) and large bath towels (wings) to enhance their performances.

● Provide books about plant life cycles. Invite children to act out the life cycles of different plants featured in the books.

A Balancing Act

Skills & Concepts

✔ **Exploring balance**

✔ **Understanding balance**

✔ **Problem solving**

Materials

■ Flat cafeteria trays (or paper box lids)

■ Plastic dinnerware items (plates, bowls, cups, forks, spoons, and so on)

Variations

Have children work in pairs. Ask one child to load the tray while the other child balances the tray on one hand. Encourage them to decide together where to place certain items to keep the tray balanced.

Rather than balancing the tray on one hand, have children balance their tray on a wooden block, creating a simple balance. Ask them to load the tray, trying to keep it from tilting to one side or the other.

How To

1 Have children create a "restaurant" using props in the dramatic play center. They might cover tables with tablecloths, add vases of flowers, and set out place settings.

2 Invite children to take the roles of customers and wait staff. Have the wait staff take food orders, serve the meal, and give the bill to their customers.

3 After their customers leave, tell the wait staff that they will clear the tables by loading the dishes onto a tray. Then show them how to balance the tray on one hand while loading dishes onto it. Explain that they should keep the tray balanced to prevent dishes from falling off.

4 As the wait staff works to keep the trays balanced, encourage them to explain their reasons for placing items in particular places on the tray. To help them problem-solve, ask questions such as: *What would happen if you put all the dishes on one side of the tray? Where is the best place to put the large dishes? Why? Is it better to stack all the same-size dishes, or to spread them out on the tray?*

5 Have children switch roles to give every child a turn to wait on customers.

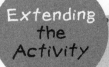

Extending the Activity

Invite children to use trays to transfer materials from one center to use in another. For example, they might load a tray with paintbrushes and paint cups (with lids tightly secured!) to take from the art center to the math center. Encourage them to use what they know about balance to load and carry the tray.

Searching for Treasure

Skills & Concepts

✔ **Predicting**

✔ **Sorting**

✔ **Exploring buoyancy**

Materials

■ Large lidded box

■ Objects to represent treasure (include items that float or sink and will fit inside the box)

■ Water table (or large container of water)

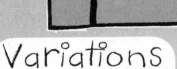

How To

1 Decorate the box and lid to resemble a treasure chest.

2 Place in the treasure chest an assortment of items to represent treasure. Be sure to include some items that float in water and some that sink. For example, you might add keys, coins, small rocks, corks, Styrofoam peanuts, and a bar of soap. Close the lid and hide the treasure chest in the dramatic play center.

3 When children visit the center, invite them to pretend they are pirates. Encourage them to assemble costumes, devise a ship, and creatively use other props to enhance their role-playing.

4 Tell the "pirates" that a treasure chest is hidden in the area. When they discover the chest, invite the pirates to open it and explore the treasures inside.

5 Ask: *What would happen if each treasure were dropped into the sea? Would it sink or float?* Invite the pirates to sort the items according to their predictions. Then have them test their predictions by placing each item in the water table.

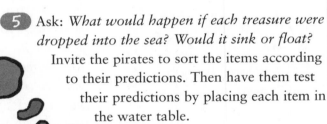

Variations

Invite each group to search the room for waterproof "treasures" that sink or float. Have the group fill the treasure chest for another group to use.

Encourage children to role-play other scenarios that might include finding treasures. For example, they might pretend to be in an attic or museum.

Extending the Activity

● Provide clue cards for children to use in their search for the treasure chest. Encourage them to follow one clue at a time until they locate the treasure.

● Fill a box the same size as the treasure chest with various objects. Have children guess which box weighs more. Let them weigh and compare the weight of each one to check their guess.

Spot the Dot!

Skills & Concepts

✔ **Matching colors**

✔ **Reasoning**

✔ **Classifying**

Materials

■ Variety of dramatic play items

■ Dot stickers in assorted colors

■ Large box

How To

1 Gather enough dramatic play items so that children can sort them into three categories, with at least five items per category. The categories might include attributes such as shape, size, texture, use, or the materials they are made of. For instance, you might gather five wooden items, five fabric items, and five plastic items.

2 Affix the same color dot sticker to each item that belongs to the same category. Use a different color for each category. (You might use red dots on the wooden items, yellow dots on the fabric items, and blue dots on the plastic items.) Place the items all around the center.

3 As children engage in dramatic play activities, encourage them to be on the lookout for items marked with colored dots. When they find one, have them put it in a designated box.

4 Before their center time ends, gather children around the box. Explain that all the items with the same dot color also have something else in common. Invite children to sort the items by the dot color. Then have them tell why all the items in each group belong together.

Variations

Give children clues to help them find the items marked with colored dots. Once all the items have been found, ask children to sort them by dot color. Then discuss the common attribute of each group.

Let children gather and group items by specific attributes. Have them apply dots to the items and then hide the items for another group to find and sort.

Extending the Activity

For each colored dot used, stick a corresponding dot on a sheet of paper. Use a separate sheet for each color. Have children count the dots on each page and then search for the items marked with that color—there will be one item per dot. Did they find all the items for each color? Can they explain why the items in each color group belong together?

What's the Weather?

Skills & Concepts

✔ Describing

✔ Classifying

✔ Understanding weather

Materials

- Posters or pictures featuring different weather conditions (several pictures for each condition)

- United States map

- Weather-related clothing and items (raincoat, rubber boots, child's safety umbrella, knit cap, mittens, large plastic shovel, sweater, tank top, sunglasses, and so on)

Variation

Display posters depicting two different kinds of weather. Have children sort out items for each kind of weather. Invite them to select items related to their choice of one of the weather conditions. Then have them act out scenes involving that weather condition.

How To

1 Display one or more posters or pictures that feature similar weather conditions. For example, you might display a poster of a snow-covered landscape, another of a snowman, and another of people skiing down a mountain. Also post the map at children's eye level.

2 Stock the dramatic play center with clothing and other items related to different kinds of weather.

3 Ask children to describe the displayed pictures. What kind of weather is represented in them? Point to areas on the map where that particular type of weather might be found. Then ask children to search the center to find clothing and items related to the pictured weather conditions. Have them put all the items for each weather condition together.

4 Have children pretend they are in a location featured in one of the pictures, or an area of the United States in which similar weather conditions exist. What will they wear? What items or tools will they need? Invite them to don clothes and gather appropriate items from those that they sorted. Then encourage them to act out activities, events, and skits related to the pictured weather conditions.

Extending the Activity

● Secretly describe to each child a particular weather condition. Ask the child to pantomime an activity related to that weather. Can classmates guess the weather?

● Fill the pockets of an apron or coat with items related to different weather conditions. Have children take turns removing an item from a pocket, naming its use, and then telling what weather condition it is used in.

Tickets, Please!

Skills & Concepts

✔ **Reading**

✔ **Writing**

✔ **Developing money skills**

Materials

■ Old movie or theater tickets

■ Large plain index cards

■ Markers

■ Stickers

■ Play money

Variations

Show children a variety of tickets such as theater and amusement park passes, bus and airline tickets, and concert tickets. Do they recognize any letters, words, or numbers on the tickets? Invite children to create and use similar kinds of tickets in their role-playing activities.

In addition to tickets, have children create posters to advertise their shows. Encourage them to include similar information on both the tickets and the posters.

How To

1 Invite children to examine the theater tickets. Ask them to point out information found on the tickets, such as the name of the show, its start time, seat assignment, ticket price, and so on. Explain that some tickets might even have a picture on them.

2 Tell children that they will perform a skit for classmates. Explain that, in addition to preparing the skit, they will also make, pass out, and collect tickets for their show.

3 On the day of their performance, give children a supply of index cards. Invite them to use markers and stickers to create tickets for their show. Encourage them to "write" the name of the show. Also have them include a picture or symbol that represents the show, the "time" of the show, and the ticket price.

4 Pass out play money to the children who are not part of the performance. Then have the performers sell their tickets to classmates. Encourage the ticket buyers to "read" the show title, time, and price on their tickets. Just before the show begins, have ticket-takers collect the tickets and seat the patrons. Lights out . . . it's show time!

Extending the Activity

● Let children count the money from their ticket sales. How much did they collect?

● Invite children to create giant-sized tickets for imaginary events. They might make tickets for pretend events such as a rainbow race or castle carnival. Encourage them to shape and decorate the tickets, as they desire, on large sheets of construction paper.

A Fabulous Flea Market

Skills & Concepts

✔ Labeling

✔ Reading

✔ Developing money skills

Materials

■ Poster board

■ Old clothing

■ Variety of dramatic play items (kitchen utensils, tools, puppets, briefcase, firefighter helmet, and so on)

■ Large sticky notes

■ Markers

■ Play money

How To

1 Write "Flea Market" in large letters on the poster board. Display the sign in the dramatic play area. Then explain to children what a flea market is.

2 Invite each group to help set up a flea market. To prepare, tell children that they will make tags for all the items to be sold at the flea market.

3 Ask children to choose several items from the collection of dramatic play items. To make tags, help them label a separate sticky note with the name of each item and its price. Ask children to attach their tags to the corresponding items.

4 After all the groups have made tags, ask a few children to help arrange the items to set up the flea market.

5 Invite two groups at a time to role-play in the flea market. Assign one group the role of sellers. Then pass out play money to the other group—the buyers. As they act out their roles, encourage children to help each other read the tags and count money for purchases.

Variation

Rather than labeling individual items, help children prepare signs to display with each category of items, such as stuffed toys, pans, and vehicles. Help them write a price on the sign that applies to each item in that category.

Extending the Activity

● Have children compare the prices of different items for sale. Which item costs the most? The least? Can they arrange three items in order by cost?

● Use marbles to represent money. Then have children draw on each tag the number of marbles that are needed to buy that item.

By the Book

Skills & Concepts

✔ **Exploring print**

✔ **Reading**

✔ **Role-playing**

Materials

- Variety of items related to a specific dramatic play theme (such as pots, pans, and measuring cups for a cooking theme)

- Books and printed materials related to a specific dramatic play theme (such as cookbooks and recipe cards)

Variations

Invite children to browse books related to a specific theme before they visit the center. Discuss the items they might use to act out activities related to the theme. Then send them to the center to gather props and begin the fun!

Provide props related to a favorite storybook, such as *The Little Engine That Could*. Invite children to "read" and then act out the story.

How To

1. Decide on a theme to emphasize in the dramatic play center. Then stock the center with items related to the theme. For example, for a cooking theme, you might supply pots, pans, mixing bowls, measuring cups and spoons, and cooking utensils.

2. Add books and other printed materials related to the theme. For a cooking theme, you might add cookbooks, recipe cards, and empty food containers printed with recipes.

3. Invite children to role-play activities related to the theme. Encourage them to use the printed materials in their play. For example, they might look up and "prepare" a recipe in a cookbook, or follow the directions on a food box.

4. As children work with the printed materials, ask questions such as: *Do you see letters or words that you know? Can you find the same word in more than one place? Can you find words with the same beginning letter as your name?*

Extending the Activity

- Help children create booklets, brochures, and pamphlets related to a specific theme. Invite them to include these materials in their role-playing activities.

- Keep the dramatic play center stocked at all times with print materials, such as cookbooks, a phone book, and old magazines. You might also include sales flyers, posters, printed refrigerator magnets, and so on.

85

What a Character!

Skills & Concepts

✔ Reading

✔ Identifying characters

✔ Expressing creativity

Materials

■ Children's favorite storybooks

■ Plain index cards

■ Markers

■ Basket

■ Dress-up clothes and accessories related to story characters

Variations

Punch a hole in each character name card and add yarn to create a necklace. Have children wear the necklaces loosely with the printed side down. Then invite them to take turns giving clues about their character. Can the group guess the character?

If desired, use only one book for this activity. Simply hold up a character name card, ask the group to "read" the name, and then have children take turns acting out an activity or trait of that character.

How To

1 Place the books and dress-up items in the dramatic play area. Let children choose several books for you to read to them. Make sure the total number of characters in the stories is at least equal to the number of children in the group.

2 After each story, discuss with children the characteristics, moods, and actions of the different characters. Then write each character's name on a separate index card and add a simple drawing of the character. Put all the cards facedown in a basket.

3 Have children take turns selecting a card and silently "reading" the name of the character. Ask them to choose dress-up clothing and accessories related to the character without revealing the character's identity.

4 Have children put on the dress-up items and then role-play the part of their character. They might act out scenes or events from the story, repeat the character's words, or tell how the character feels. Can classmates guess which character each child represents?

THE THREE LITTLE PIGS

Extending the Activity

Print on chart paper different emotions experienced by characters in the stories. Draw a simple face to represent each emotion. Encourage children to include emotions in the dramatizations of their character. Have classmates try to identify each emotion being displayed and then find the word for that emotion on the chart.

Picture Perfect

Skills & Concepts

✔ **Exploring emotions**
✔ **Reading**
✔ **Matching**

Materials

■ Pictures of people expressing different emotions

■ Scissors

■ 9- by 12-inch construction paper

■ Glue

■ Plain index cards

■ Marker

Variations

Reverse the activity! Show children a word card and have them find all the pictures that are labeled with a matching word. Help them read the word. Then invite them to express that emotion in their own way.

Invite children to sort the pictures by the emotions represented in them, match each word card to the corresponding group of pictures, and then demonstrate one expression of each emotion.

How To

1 Cut out pictures of people expressing different emotions. You might find pictures in brochures, sales flyers, magazines, old posters, and so on. Look for pictures that feature individuals and groups of people.

2 Glue each picture to a separate sheet of construction paper. Label each page with the word for the emotion being expressed in the picture. When finished, label one index card for each different emotion represented by the pictures. For example, you might have four pictures labeled "happy," but you will write "happy" on only one index card.

3 Display the word cards on a table. Then show children one picture at a time. Ask a child to "read" the picture by describing the emotion shown by the person or people in it. Can the child read the word on the page? After helping the child identify the word, have him or her find the card with the matching word.

4 To end his or her turn, invite the child to pantomime the emotion depicted in the picture.

Extending the Activity

Show children pictures that feature people engaged in activities such as celebrating a birthday, walking a dog, riding in a car, and playing a sport. Have children take turns choosing a picture to "read" and then role-playing the activity and related emotion.

What Can It Be?

Skills & Concepts

✔ **Cooperating**

✔ **Developing fine motor skills**

✔ **Expressing creativity**

Materials

■ White full-size bedsheet (one for every four groups of children)

■ Large sheet of cardboard (or several sheets of poster board)

■ Fabric paint

■ Paintbrushes

■ Assorted dramatic play items that can be used with paint (plastic forks, combs, cups, and so on)

Variations

Invite children to plan a sequence of uses for the decorated sheet. For instance, they might use it as a picnic blanket, then as a tent, and, later, as a stage curtain.

Divide each quarter-section of the sheet into several smaller sections. Invite pairs of children to plan and decorate each smaller section.

How To

1 Fold the sheet in half twice so that it is one-fourth of its original size. Insert a large sheet of cardboard under the top layer of the sheet (this will protect the bottom layers as children paint the top layer).

2 Explain that children will decide together how to decorate their section of the sheet. They might paint colored stripes, smiley faces, or bold shapes. Or they might paint a scene with trees, grass, and flowers. Show them the collection of items. Tell them that they can use any of these as "paintbrushes."

3 Have children decorate the sheet as planned. Encourage them to use the pretend paintbrushes to add interest to their designs.

4 When the paint dries, refold the sheet so that an unpainted section is on top. Invite the next group to paint that section.

5 After the entire sheet has been decorated, invite groups to decide how they can use it in their play activities. They might use it as a tent, tablecloth, picnic blanket, or cape.

Extending the Activity

● To promote quick thinking and gross motor skills, have children use the sheet in a parachute toss game. They might use the "parachute" to toss balloons or foam balls.

● Add the decorated sheet to the classroom library. Invite children to sit on it as they enjoy their favorite books. Or display the sheet in the classroom for children to enjoy.

Art

Sounds Like a Parade!

Skills & Concepts

✔ Describing
✔ Listening
✔ Identifying instruments

Materials

■ Rhythm band instruments
■ Dress-up clothes

Variations

Bring in a variety of instruments new to children. After they explore the sounds each one makes, have children sit in a circle with their eyes closed. Then challenge them to guess which instrument they hear as you play each one.

Fill two boxes with identical items. Use items from the dramatic play center that can be used to create music (pans, spoons, cans, and so on). Give children one box. Then, behind a screen, remove two items from the other box and play a rhythm with them. Can children find the same two items from their box and duplicate the rhythm?

How To

1. Invite children to tell about their experiences watching or participating in parades. Encourage them to describe the sounds related to parades, such as bands playing, drums beating, clapping, cheering, and shouting.

2. Explain that children will take part in a musical parade around the classroom. Invite them to choose clothes and hats from the dramatic play center to wear during the parade.

3. When children are dressed and ready, seat them in a circle. Tell them that they will each be given an instrument to play in the parade.

4. To pass out the instruments, have children close their eyes. Then walk around the circle with an instrument. Stop behind a child and softly play the instrument above his or her head. Can the child identify the instrument? If needed, invite classmates to help him or her guess. Then give the instrument to the child.

5. When each child has received an instrument, invite the group to stand up, play the instruments, and parade around the room to their own marching music.

Extending the Activity

Provide oatmeal boxes, chip canisters, shoe boxes, lidded yogurt cups, and an assortment of craft supplies. Have children create their own instruments to use in a class parade.

Check Out the Scenery!

Skills & Concepts

✔ Cooperating

✔ Developing fine motor skills

✔ Expressing creativity

Materials

■ Lengths of white bulletin board paper (one per group)

■ Paint

■ Paintbrushes

■ Markers

Variations

Encourage children to use their imaginations to create wallpaper backdrops that feature flowers, colorful designs, or even letters!

Create an interactive scene! Simply have children trace their bodies onto the bulletin board paper. Cut out a circle from each head. Then have children decorate the bodies and scenery. When finished, display the backdrop so that children can stand behind it and peer through the openings.

How To

1 Discuss some of the themes that children might role-play in the dramatic play center. Then have them choose one theme that they would like to make a backdrop for. For example, they might want to create a fire station scene to use in their fire-fighting role-playing.

2 Give children a length of bulletin board paper, paint, paintbrushes, and markers. Have them work together to plan what kinds of things will be included in their backdrop. For a fire station scene, they might include the garage, fire trucks, fire poles, and a few firefighters. After agreeing on the elements of their backdrop, have children decorate their scene.

3 When the paint dries, display the group's backdrop in the dramatic play center. Then invite the group to enjoy role-playing activities related to the theme. Encourage them to incorporate the scenery into their play.

4 Before children leave the center, help them carefully take down their scene, roll it up, secure it with a rubber band, and set it aside. Then, the next time that group—or another group—engages in activities related to that theme, display the scene to enhance their role-playing fun.

Extending the Activity

Provide children with a length of bulletin board paper. Help them draw and cut out costumes related to their dramatic play activities. They can use clothespins, yarn, or tape to fasten on their costumes. What a perfect fit for role-playing fun!

A Little Background Music

Skills & Concepts

✔ **Following directions**
✔ **Developing rhythm**
✔ **Expressing creativity**

Materials

■ Masking tape
■ Rhythm band instruments
■ Large wooden spoon
■ Dramatic play props and costumes

Variations

In secret, ask the performer to take the role of something that moves in a rhythmic pattern, such as a horse or train. Have the conductor lead the musicians in following the performer's rhythmic movements. Can the musicians guess what the performer represents?

Ask the conductor to lead the musicians in creating action or mood music, such as rhythms that "hop," "run," or sound happy or sad. Invite volunteers to perform to each rhythm.

How To

1 Tape off an area of the floor to use as an "orchestra pit." Place the instruments in the orchestra pit. Explain to children that an orchestra pit is where musicians sit during theater performances.

2 Tell children that the orchestra leader is called a conductor. Then, using the wooden spoon as a baton, demonstrate how the conductor leads the musicians.

3 Invite children to enter the orchestra pit, select an instrument, and sit down. Posing as the conductor, lead children in a few rounds of music making. Encourage them to watch you for cues to start playing their instruments, to know how fast (or slow) to play, and when to stop. Then let children take turns being the conductor.

4 Add a theatrical performance to the music. Invite a child to dress up as a particular character, such as a prince or princess. Ask the character to stand in front of the orchestra pit. Then have the conductor lead the musicians in a round of music while the character moves about to interpret the music.

Extending the Activity

Reverse the activity! Invite one child to play a rhythm while the other children perform to the music. Encourage each performer to notice how the others interpret the music.

Mailbox Make-Believe

Skills & Concepts

✔ Writing

✔ Matching names

✔ Expressing creativity

Materials

■ Empty tissue boxes (one per child)

■ Paint and paintbrushes

■ Stickers

■ Large and small index cards

■ Paper and envelopes

■ Dress-up clothes and props related to a letter-carrier theme

How To

1 To make mailboxes, have children paint their tissue boxes the color of their choice. When dry, invite them to decorate the mailboxes with stickers. Attach an index card labeled with each child's name to his or her mailbox.

2 Have children set up their mailboxes around the dramatic play center. Then invite them to "write" letters and postcards to other children in their group. Help them to address each piece of mail with the recipient's name. Make sure they leave envelopes unsealed so that they can be reused.

3 Invite a child to be the letter carrier. Have the letter carrier pack all the mail into a bag and then deliver it by matching the name on each piece to the name on a mailbox. After the mail run, have children empty the mailboxes and "read" their mail.

4 Ask children to return their letters to the envelopes. Then collect all the mail in the mail bag. Repeat the activity until each child has had a turn to be the letter carrier.

Variation

Label each child's mailbox with the name of a community worker. Then help children address mail to the different community workers (instead of to specific children). After the letter carrier delivers the mail, invite each child to "read" the mail delivered to his or her community worker.

Extending the Activity

● Expand the play area by taping a road that winds into and out of the center. (If space allows, you might add a few roads that branch off the main one.) Have children place their mailboxes on stacked-block mailbox posts along the road.

● Encourage children to work together to create a country scene for their mail route. For example, they might paint a length of bulletin board paper with trees, birds, small animals, barns, and so on. Display the scene in the dramatic play center.

BLOCK CENTER

MY CASTLE

hroughout this section, you'll find ideas for introducing math, science, art, dramatic play, and literacy-building experiences into your block center. Each activity uses the existing materials in your block center to explore not only math concepts such as measuring, estimating, shape and size recognition, patterning, and one-to-one correspondence, but also concepts related to science, art, dramatic play, and literacy. Use blocks for print-making experiences? For estimating heights and weights? For theatrical performances? Why not? Blocks can be used in unlimited ways to extend learning into other curriculum areas. Just remember, when you open your learning center to the possibility of reinforcing skills from science to art, more than building can happen in the block center!

Blocks for All Seasons

Whatever the weather, your block center can reflect the mood and activities that make each season special.

Autumn Activities

Have children cut circles from orange construction paper to represent pumpkins. Help children arrange the paper pumpkins in rows on the floor. Then invite them to divide the rows with blocks to create a classroom pumpkin patch!

Visit an apple orchard and return to the classroom with a bushel of apples. Place each apple in a resealable plastic sandwich bag. Then have children build a block "apple" tree on the floor. Have them place the apples near the tree branches as if hanging from the tree. Later, let children "pick" the apples, rinse them, and enjoy a delicious snack!

Place a collection of gourds and small pumpkins in your block center. Use the foods to create a simple ABC pattern (such as gourd, gourd, pumpkin, gourd, gourd, pumpkin). Invite children to try to replicate the pattern with different shaped blocks to represent the foods.

Create a giant cornucopia by rolling a length of bulletin board paper. Place it on the floor in your block area. Have children estimate how many of one particular kind of block will fill the cornucopia. Invite children to fill the cornucopia to test their estimates.

Winter Activities

Cut three large circles (of the same size) from white construction paper. Arrange the circles on the floor of the block area to represent a snow person. Ask children to estimate how many blocks of one particular size it will take to fill each part of the snow person's body. Have children cover each circle with blocks to test their estimates.

Invite children to create igloos with blocks. As they gather together to keep warm inside their igloos, share stories with children about warm weather climates to help "warm" them up!

Have children paint a winter scene on a large sheet of bulletin board paper. Hang the mural as a backdrop to your block area. As children build with blocks, encourage them to create block structures in the shape of sleds, snow people, and so on.

Enjoy some winter fun by taking an imaginary sleigh ride! Work with children to create a large rectangle outline from blocks. Later, have small groups of children take turns sitting in the "sleigh" and describing what they "see" as the imaginary sleigh goes up and down snow-covered hills and valleys.

Spring Activities

Help children create flower stems with blocks. Then offer construction paper, scissors, and glue so children can create their own colorful blossoms. Print children's names on the blossoms, and have them place flowers on top of the block stems. Later, stroll through this lovely block garden with children. Encourage each child to describe his or her flower to the others in the group.

Share picture books that feature diamond shapes. Then have children hunt for diamond-shaped objects around the room. Explain that kites are often diamond shaped. Invite children to create diamond-shaped kites with blocks, adding lengths of ribbon or yarn to represent kite tails. Later, on a breezy day, go kite-flying outdoors with children.

Go on an outdoor twig hunt with children. Back inside, explain that birds use twigs, along with leaves and grass, to build their nests. Invite children to build giant bird nests with blocks, using the twigs to enhance their nests. Later, have children pretend to be birds chirping and flapping their "wings" as they enjoy their new homes.

Invite children to create circles of blocks to represent puddles. Then help them build gross motor skills as they follow your directions to jump over a puddle, hop on one foot into a puddle, skip around a puddle, and so on.

Summer Activities

Have children create a large block circle to represent pond. Ask them to cut out construction-paper fish, tape a paper clip to the back of each fish, and put it in the "pond." Give children a wooden-dowel fishing rod that has a magnet attached to the end of the fishing line. Then invite them to take turns fishing in the pond!

Invite children to create a large almond shape with blocks to represent a rowboat. When finished, discuss summer safety rules, including wearing life jackets when boating. Then invite them to pantomime putting on their life jackets, choosing their oars, and climbing into the boat. As they take the boat for an imaginary spin around the block center, invite children to sing "Row, Row, Row Your Boat."

Outdoors, spread a large sheet of bulletin board paper on the ground. Have children paint glue all over the paper and then sprinkle sand on the glue. When dry, shake off the excess sand and bring the paper "beach" into your block area. Invite children to build pretend sand castles, made from blocks, on this sandy beach.

"On the Spot"

Block Center Celebrations

Hold a "Block Party." Talk with children about the special places they like to visit in their own neighborhoods. Then encourage each child to replicate one of these places with blocks. Help children create tagboard labels for their block buildings. When finished, invite them take a walk around their block "neighborhood."

Use blocks to lead children to a special surprise! While children are at an activity in another part of school, create a block pathway that leads from the block center to a "surprise" activity set up in another area of the room. The surprise might be an exciting science experiment, interesting art activity, or a feely bag activity. When children return, invite them to follow the path to the surprise that awaits them. Each time you enjoy this celebration, make the block pathway a bit more difficult to follow!

Make a wish! Build a wishing well in your block area. Keep the well low enough so that children can easily place a "wishing block" inside it. Then ask: *What is your special wish?* Print each child's wish on an index card, tape it to a block, and have him or her place it inside the well. Later in the year review children's wishes. Are these wishes still important to children? Would they wish for other things instead?

Celebrate children's growth! From time to time, have children work in pairs to measure their height with blocks. To do this, ask one child to lie on the floor with his or her heels just barely touching the wall. Have his or her partner line up blocks alongside the child from head to foot, using blocks that are all the same size. When finished, have the pair count the blocks used to measure the child's height. Record the results, child's name, and date on an index card. Then have the partners switch roles. At the end of the activity, collect the cards. Later in the year, repeat the activity and have children compare their new heights to those on the cards you collected.

Invite children to play Memory with your blocks! Collect 20 blocks all in the same size and shape. Then cut out ten pairs of different shapes from construction paper. Tape each shape onto a separate block. Place all the blocks shape side down on a table and have children use the block "cards" to play Memory.

Recyclable Materials
for the Block Center

Here are some recyclable materials you'll want to have on hand to add interest and surprise to your block area.

Science and Math in the Block Center

Materials	Possible Use
Empty seed packages	for use in "block gardens"
Egg cartons	for sorting small blocks
Ribbon and yarn	for pulley systems and push/pull experiments
Aluminum pie plates and baking pans	for float/sink activities
Paper plates	to display in block buildings to make clocks
Clean, empty popcorn buckets	to fill with blocks and use in weight or balance activities

Literacy in the Block Center

Materials	Possible Use
Old telephone books	to use in block homes
Paper scraps and sticky notes	for making signs and labels for block structures
Old computer keyboards	to accompany "computers" built with blocks
Junk mail	to deliver to block houses in post office play
Travel brochures	for airport play with blocks

Art and Dramatic Play in the Block Center

Materials	Possible Use
Packaging paper	to wrap blocks and use for block-printing activities
Tissue boxes	for planters on block homes
Paper towel tubes	for telescopes to use in block buildings
Old menus and telephones	for restaurant play in block area
Scraps of ribbon, lace, and fabric	to use to wrap or decorate block "gifts"
Cardboard pizza rounds	for steering wheels on block vehicles

Measure for Measure

Skills & Concepts

✔ Developing fine motor skills

✔ Measuring

✔ Counting

Materials

■ Newsprint or large sheets of construction paper

■ Markers

■ Scissors

■ Blocks

■ Chart paper

How To

1 Have children work in pairs. Invite one child in each pair to remove his or her shoes and step on the newsprint or construction paper. The child's partner will trace each of his or her feet five times to make five pairs of footprints. Then have children switch roles. Label each footprint with the name or initials of the child.

2 Help children cut out their five pairs of footprints.

3 Invite children to build freely in the block area (independently or in small groups). As children finish their creations, tell them that they will measure each one using their own footprints as a measuring tool.

4 Show children how to lay the footprints toe to heel against their block structure to measure its length and width. Have them work with a partner to hold the footprints end to end to measure the height.

5 On chart paper, record how many footprints long, wide, and high each child's block structure is.

Variations

Have children use their handprints, rather than footprints, to measure their block buildings.

Instead of using footprints, have children walk heel to toe around their block buildings to determine how many "feet" long or wide each block building is.

Extending the Activity

● Have children compare their block structure measurements on the chart paper. Ask: *Whose building is the longest? Highest? Widest?*

● Invite children to search the classroom (and, if you choose, outdoor space as well) for other objects to measure with their footprints. You might ask: *How long is the balance beam? How high is the easel? How wide is the doll cradle?*

You're Blocking My View!

Skills & Concepts

✔ **Estimating**

✔ **Developing fine motor skills**

✔ **Counting**

Materials

■ *Caps for Sale* by Esphyr Slobodkina (Harper Trophy, 1987)

■ Masking tape

■ Collection of hats from dramatic play area (including firefighter helmet, police officer cap, and chef hat)

■ Square or rectangular blocks (all the same size)

How To

1 Read *Caps for Sale* with children. Have them count the number of caps they see on different pages. Point out the different heights of the stacks of caps.

2 Tape a line to the floor in the block area. Place the collection of hats behind the line. Have all the children sit in front of the line.

3 Invite a builder and an estimator up to the line. Ask the builder to build a stack of hats behind the line. Then have the estimator estimate how many blocks it will take to block the hats from the other children's view.

4 Have the builder build a block tower on the line, making it high enough to block the stack of hats from the group's view. Then have the estimator count the blocks to check the accuracy of his or her estimate.

Variation

Supply children with small, medium, and large blocks. After they have blocked classmates' view of the hats with one size block, have them build a tower using another block size. Ask: *Will more or fewer of the smaller blocks be required to hide the hats? Will more or fewer of the larger blocks be needed?*

Extending the Activity

● Invite children to build block homes for plastic or stuffed figures (people and animals). Encourage them to estimate how many blocks it will take to build a home for the people or animals.

● Have a group of children work together to build a block structure. When finished, invite a second group to estimate how many blocks it will take to copy the structure. Then have the group replicate the structure to test its estimate.

Getting in Shape

Skills & Concepts

✔ **Recognizing shapes**

✔ **Forming shapes**

✔ **Developing gross motor skills**

Materials

■ Blocks in all shapes and sizes

How To

1 Have children sit with you in the block area to examine the blocks. Together, name the shapes, count the number of sides, discuss the ways in which the shapes are the same and different, and identify other objects that have similar shapes.

2 Invite children to work together to create a large circle with blocks. Then have them make a circle with their bodies, using their block circle as a guide. Children might join hands around the block circle, or lie on the floor so that their heads and feet nearly touch those of their classmates to make a ring around the circle.

3 Continue the activity by having children use different blocks, and then their bodies, to represent other shapes, such as a square, triangle, diamond, and rectangle.

Variation

Invite children to work together in small groups to form letters with their bodies. Then see if other children can identify the letters.

Extending the Activity

● Have children look around the room for objects of different shapes (plastic starfish, oval-shaped pillow, long rectangular scarf, round ball, and so on). Challenge them to construct these shapes with blocks.

● If possible, take instant pictures of children's block shapes. Distribute the photos and then have children gather objects around the classroom that have matching shapes.

Count 'n' Build

Skills & Concepts
✔ Following directions
✔ Recognizing shapes
✔ Recognizing numerals

Materials
■ Chart paper
■ Markers
■ Blocks

How To

1 Make a "block-building guide" on chart paper. Use rebus shapes so that children can read the chart independently. It might look like the chart below.

2 Display the block-building guide in the block center. To use, have children count out the number of each kind of block indicated on the guide. Then invite them to build their own original structures with the blocks.

3 When finished, have children compare their structures to those built by their classmates. Each one will look different, even though they all used the same kinds of blocks!

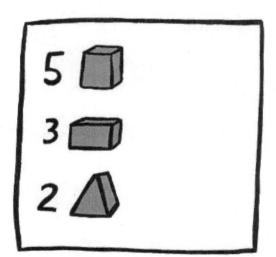

Variations

Try using a magnetic board for this activity. Use magnetic numerals and simple construction paper cutouts representing the different blocks to create block-building guides.

As children become familiar with the activity, replace the numerals with sets of lines or dots to represent the numbers. Children can count these to see how many of each type of block to use.

Extending the Activity

Let children create building guides for their classmates. Encourage each child to read his or her guide to the builders before they begin working on their structures.

A Tower of Power

Skills & Concepts
✔ Comparing
✔ Exploring balance
✔ Exploring gravity

Materials
■ Blocks in various shapes and sizes

How To

1 Build two block towers, one that might topple over easily and another that is stronger and more stable. Ask: *What is the difference between the two towers? How does the construction of the stronger tower help it stay up?*

2 Invite children to build the tallest tower they can with a small set of blocks. When finished, ask: *How sturdy is your tower? What could someone do to topple your tower? Would it be difficult to topple? Would it be easy to topple?*

3 Explain that you are going to build several additional towers. When finished, have children gather around one tower at a time. Starting with the tower they built, ask children: *What could you do to strengthen this tower with other blocks?* After sharing, let children test their ideas. They might add larger blocks to the bottom of the tower to strengthen the foundation, add side supports with additional block towers, or add width to the tower to provide reinforcement.

4 After working with each tower, discuss with children why their ideas did or didn't work. Also, invite them to share what they have learned about balance and gravity in this activity.

Variation

If using wooden blocks, try the same activity with blocks made of different materials (cardboard, sponge, foam, or plastic).

Extending the Activity

● Provide other objects or building materials children might use to strengthen their towers. How can they use large sheets of cardboard? Plastic buckets? Doll furniture from the dramatic play area?

● Bring a collection of relatively tall objects into the block area. You might include a toy broom-stand, a stand-up doll, or a toy high chair. Invite children to create sturdy block structures to house the objects.

Homes by the Block

Skills & Concepts

✔ Exploring animal homes

✔ Developing fine motor skills

✔ Describing shape and size

Materials

■ Masking tape

■ *Animal Homes* by Angela Wilkes (Kingfisher, 2003)

■ Animal pictures or stickers

■ Index cards

■ Shoe box

■ Blocks

Variation

Reverse the activity. Have children build animal homes of their own choosing. Later, without naming the animal that would live in each home, have children describe their homes to the group. See if the other children can identify the animal that would live in each home.

How To

1 Explain that children will create a special kind of neighborhood. Use masking tape to mark off a square on the floor large enough for each child to construct a block animal home within the square.

2 Share *Animal Homes* with children. Discuss how each home is suited to the specific needs of the animal.

3 Make animal cards by attaching a different animal picture or sticker to an index card. Place the cards facedown in the shoe box.

4 Let each child pick a card from the box. Discuss the animal on each child's card. Ask: *What kind of home might this animal have? Does it live in a nest? A cave? A doghouse? An underground home?*

5 Have each child create a block home for the animal on his or her card. Then tape the card to home. Ask the child to describe the animal home and then tell how it is appropriate for his or her animal.

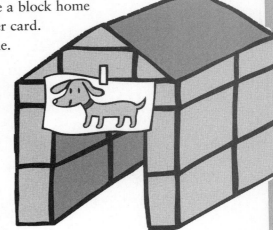

Extending the Activity

Provide additional materials so children can add details to their animal homes. You might offer sticks and twigs for "nests" or plastic containers to represent food and water bowls.

103

A Rock in the Blocks!

Skills & Concepts

✔ **Observing nature**

✔ **Classifying**

✔ **Reasoning**

Materials

■ Blocks

■ Paper bags (one per child)

■ Objects found in nature, including rocks, leaves, twigs, acorns, weeds, flowers, and small plants

How To

1 Take children on a nature walk. Encourage them to look up, down, and all around as they enjoy the wonder of the great outdoors. Then distribute the paper bags. Have children collect objects that interest them, such as pinecones, pebbles and rocks, leaves, moss, grass, and so on.

2 Back in the classroom, gather a group of children in the block center. Have them work together to make three large squares with blocks. In the first square, place a few rocks; in the second, a few blades of grass; and in the third, several leaves.

3 Invite children to remove the contents of their bags, and place each object in a square in which they think it belongs. For instance, they might place pebbles in the rock square, weeds in the grass square, and twigs in the leaf square.

4 When finished, let children describe the items within each square. Have them explain why they categorized the items as they did.

Variation

Invite children to collect only one type of object outdoors. They might collect only rocks, weeds, leaves, or grasses. Then encourage children to sort their items based on detailed differences such as size or color. For instance, they might sort leaves by whether they are dark, medium, or light green.

Extending the Activity

Have each child place one of his or her collected items on a single block as a way to "feature" it. Have children gather around the block as the child describes, in as much detail as possible, the featured item. He or she might describe the color and texture of the object, where it was found, what makes it different from the other collected objects, or how it might change as time goes on.

Buckets of Blocks

Skills & Concepts

✔ **Exploring volume**

✔ **Exploring weight**

✔ **Estimating**

Materials

■ Two large plastic buckets (of the same size and weight)

■ Blocks

■ Bathroom scale

■ Index cards

■ Markers

How To

1 Sit together as a group. Have two children volunteer to each fill a different bucket with blocks. They can fill the buckets in any way they like: with blocks all in one size or shape, or in any combination of their choosing.

2 Invite children to examine the contents of both buckets and estimate which weighs more. Encourage them to explain reasons for their estimates (size of blocks, number of blocks, weight of individual blocks, and so on).

3 To check children's estimates, have one of the volunteers place his or her bucket on the scale. Record the weight on an index card. Then invite the second volunteer to place his or her bucket on the scale. Record the weight of that bucket on another card. Show children the cards and ask: *Which bucket of blocks weighs more?* Have children recall their estimates and compare them to the results. Were their estimates correct?

Variation

Do the same activity using containers smaller than the buckets. Encourage children to describe how the size of the container affects the weights. Ask: *What do you think would happen if you used containers that are larger than the buckets?*

Extending the Activity

● After weighing the buckets of blocks, encourage children to consider ways they could increase and decrease the weights of the buckets. Invite them to test their ideas.

● Invite children to try to make both buckets weigh the same. Ask: *Which kinds of blocks will you use? Do you need to use the same blocks in each bucket? If you put a big, heavy block in one bucket, how many lighter, smaller ones do you think you'll need to put in the other?*

Take Me to the Toy Shop

Skills & Concepts

✔ **Describing objects**

✔ **Matching words to objects**

✔ **Role-playing**

Materials

■ Blocks

■ Poster board

■ Collection of toys

■ Index cards

■ Markers

■ Toy cash register

■ Play money

Variations

Change the type of shop that children create. They might set up a bakery, shoe store, clothing shop, and so on. Help children create appropriate labels for items in the shop.

Add a large box to represent a shopping basket. Then ask children to "purchase" a certain number of toys. After "shopping," have them count the items to make sure they have selected the correct number.

How To

1 Talk with children about their experiences visiting toy stores. Ask: *What kinds of toys might you find at a toy store? How might they be displayed?*

2 Explain that children will help build a toy shop in the block area. Then have them use blocks to build shelves for the shop's toy collection.

3 Brainstorm a name for the shop with children. Print the name on a poster board and display it in the block area.

4 Have children place classroom toys on the "toy shop" shelves. As they work, ask children to name and describe each toy. Print the toy names on individual index cards. Then help children to "read" and match each card to the corresponding toy.

5 Add a cash register and play money. Invite children to pretend to shop in their special toy shop.

Extending the Activity

● Create price tags for the different items on the toy store shelves. Help children determine how much play money they will need to purchase specific items.

● Have children sort and categorize the toys. You might have them place toys with moving parts in one area, toys made of soft fabrics in another, and toy vehicles in another.

Fill It In!

Skills & Concepts

✔ **Identifying letters**

✔ **Forming letters**

✔ **Developing fine motor skills**

Materials

■ Blocks

■ Masking tape

■ Alphabet chart

■ Small toy vehicles or figures (such as plastic animals or people)

How To

1 Display an alphabet chart at children's eye level in the block center.

2 Tape a large outline of any letter on the floor. Then have children gather at the base of the letter. Ask them to name the letter. Discuss the letter's shape. Invite children to find the letter on the alphabet chart.

3 Invite children to place blocks on top of the masking tape outline to form the letter. When finished, have children stand back and look at the block letter that they created.

4 To reinforce the letter's shape, have children "trace" the letter by rolling small toy vehicles or walking small plastic animals or human figures along the blocks that form the letter.

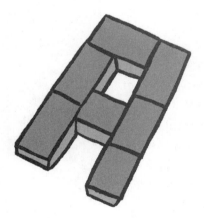

Variations

● Create children's initials with masking tape. Have them use blocks to form each letter on top of its outline.

● Cut out large letter outlines from lightweight cardboard. Attach the cardboard letter to the floor with masking tape. Have children fill in the outlines with blocks to make block letters.

Extending the Activity

● Cover a block letter with a large sheet of white paper. Have children make a crayon rubbing of the letter, being careful not to shift the blocks as they work.

● Take instant photos of children's block letters. Have children arrange the photos in alphabetical order and then use the alphabet chart to check their work.

Literacy

What's in a Name?

Skills & Concepts

✔ **Recognizing letters**

✔ **Recognizing names**

✔ **Expressing creativity**

Materials

■ Sheet of chart paper

■ Markers

■ Blocks

How To

1 Print each child's first and last name on the chart paper. Underline their initials.

2 In the block center, label each section of the block shelves, or sections of the block storage area, with a different letter.

3 Review with children the names on the chart paper. Discuss which children have similar letters in their names.

4 Invite children to build with blocks from those shelves or sections that are labeled with the letters found in their initials.

Variations

Print numerals on index cards and use them as labels in the block storage area. Children can count the number of letters in their names, find those number cards, and then use the blocks in those sections to create block structures.

Print several children's names on index cards and tape them to the floor in the block area. Invite these children to locate their names and build block structures beside their names.

Extending the Activity

● After children have finished building, help them create labels for their block structures. They might label the structures with their names, an invented word, or the actual name of what their structure represents.

● Encourage children to dictate stories about their block structures. Print their dictations on chart paper. Then display each story beside the appropriate block structure. As children share their structures with one another, read their stories to the group.

● Make individual name cards for children and place them in an envelope. As each child builds a block structure, help another child in the group find the builder's name in the envelope and attach it to the structure.

Build Block Letters

Skills & Concepts

✔ **Recognizing letters**
✔ **Forming letters**
✔ **Comparing**

Materials

■ Chalkboard or write-on/wipe-off board and marker

■ Wooden or cardboard blocks

■ Small wooden or plastic blocks

How To

1 Bring a portable chalkboard or write-on/wipe-off board into the block center. Print a large letter on the board.

2 Talk with children about the letter. Ask: *How many lines do you see in the letter? Are all the lines the same length? What shape does the letter resemble? Does it resemble a circle, triangle, square, or rectangle?*

3 Invite children to use small blocks from the manipulatives area and large wooden or cardboard blocks from the block area to create models of the letter. They might stack the blocks to make a thick letter or use the small blocks to make tiny representations of the letter. When finished, have children compare their letters. Ask: *How are they all the same? How are they different? Which is the largest or smallest letter?*

Variations

Use masking tape to make a large letter on the floor. Invite children to place blocks on the outline to make a large block letter.

Invite children to work together to make the largest representations of the letters that they can. (Be careful! Once children get started, you might discover a letter that covers the entire classroom floor!)

Extending the Activity

● As children experience success with creating block letters, print simple words on the board and then have children duplicate the words with blocks.

● Gather classroom items that begin with the featured letter. For instance, when working with the letter *b*, you might collect a ball, paper butterfly, plastic bug, small blanket, and so on. Then show children each item. Have them name the item and tell what letter sound it begins with.

It's on the Web!

Skills & Concepts

✔ Cooperating

✔ Matching numbers

✔ Role-playing

Materials

■ Blocks

■ Two sets of numeral cards (with 1–10 printed on the individual cards)

How To

1 Work with children to build a large spiderweb on the floor with blocks. Leave room so that one child can walk into the web and stand at the center.

2 Invite children to sit in a circle around the web. Distribute one set of the numeral cards, one card to each child.

3 Hold up a numeral card from the second set of cards. Have the child with the matching card move to the center of the web.

4 Ask the remaining children to sing "The Eensy Weensy Spider." As they sing, have children dramatize the actions of the song. Each time they sing the words "the eensy weensy spider," have them point to the "spider" standing in the center of the web.

Variation

Add pictures of farm animals to the number cards. Together, build an outline of a block barn. Then sing "Old MacDonald." When you name a farm animal, the child with the matching animal on his or her card will step into the block barn and make that animal's sound at the appropriate time in the song. (For example, the child with a picture of a cow on his or her card will say, "Moo, Moo" when you sing "With a *moo, moo* here and a *moo, moo* there.")

Extending the Activity

Place a different numeral card on each "spoke" of the block spiderweb. Assign each child to a spoke of the web. Then give children paper bags and have them collect objects around the room that represent the numbers on their spokes. When finished, have children sit near their spokes. As they share the contents of their bags, have children count the items to verify that they have collected the correct number.

Wrap It Up!

Skills & Concepts

✔ Developing fine motor skills

✔ Identifying colors

✔ Expressing creativity

Materials

■ Small- and medium-sized blocks

■ Sheet of newsprint or newspaper (one per child)

■ Masking tape

■ Bulletin board paper

■ Tempera paint in different colors

■ Plastic or Styrofoam plates (for paint trays)

■ Paper towels

How To

1. Cover the floor of your block area with newspaper. Have each child select a small- to medium-sized block.

2. Explain that you will help children wrap their blocks in a piece of newsprint. Work with each child to help him or her tightly wrap the paper around a block. Tape the paper in place to create a carefully covered "block package."

3. Lay a large sheet of bulletin board paper on the floor. Place a supply of paper towels nearby for clean-up purposes.

4. To make a giant block-print collage, invite children to lightly dip their paper-covered blocks in paint and press them onto the paper. Then have them name the color of their block print.

5. As children work, invite them to turn their blocks, dip an unused side into a different color of paint, and then print that side of the block onto the paper. Emphasize that they can use all sides of their blocks for printing.

6. When dry, display the prints for all to enjoy.

Variation

Invite children to wrap the blocks with bubble wrap or pieces of textured fabric to create interesting print effects.

Extending the Activity

● Invite children to add prints of other classroom objects.

● Carefully unwrap the blocks and let the paper dry. Later, see if children can identify the block that had been wrapped in each piece of paper.

All Around the Block

Skills & Concepts

✔ Developing fine motor skills

✔ Recognizing shapes

✔ Expressing creativity

Materials

■ 12- by 18-inch white construction paper (one sheet per child)

■ Blocks

■ Crayons

How To

1 For each child, lay one sheet of construction paper on the floor of your block area.

2 Invite children to select a block to trace onto their paper.

3 When finished, have children take a close look at the shape on the paper. Ask: *What do you think the shape might be? What can you make from this shape?*

4 Using the block shape as a starting point, invite children to draw a design, person, or object on the paper. A square shape might be the start of a special birthday package, with a surrounding birthday party setting. A curved shape might be a piece of an imaginative machine. A large rectangular shape might be a seesaw.

5 Invite children to share their drawings with the group. Ask the other children to try to identify the block shape that inspired the original creation.

Variation

Have children work in small groups. Invite each child to trace a different block onto the same sheet of bulletin board paper. Then have them work together to create a piece of art from all the shapes on the paper.

Extending the Activity

● Provide additional art supplies, including glue, paint, fabric scraps, ribbon, yarn, and glitter so children can add detail, texture, and color to their drawings.

● Encourage children to dictate stories about their block-shape drawings. Print children's dictations on chart paper. Display the stories, along with children's block artwork, on a classroom wall or bulletin board.

Beautiful Block Sculptures

Skills & Concepts

✔ **Exploring shapes**
✔ **Exploring size**
✔ **Expressing creativity**

Materials

■ Art books with various photographs of sculptures

■ Posters of sculptures

■ Blocks

How To

1 Explore the art books and posters with children. Encourage children to talk about which sculptures they like, which they don't like, and why.

2 Invite children to create their own sculptures with blocks. As children select their blocks, have them examine the differences among the blocks, and consider how they might be combined to create original sculptures.

3 After the block sculptures are completed, give each child an opportunity to describe his or her sculpture to the rest of the group. Have large sticky notes handy in case children want to "title" and sign their artwork!

Variations

Invite children to reuse large pieces of Styrofoam to create their sculptures. You can also provide colorful beads, pipe cleaners, and so on, for children to add color and detail to their sculptures.

Place several decorative posters on the floor. Invite children to use blocks to create interesting frames for the posters.

Extending the Activity

● Invite children to draw pictures of their block sculptures so that, once disassembled, the sculptures will live on! Display the drawings in the block area.

● Have children create sculptures from clay or play dough. As they create, encourage children to discuss how working with the clay or play dough is both similar to and different from working with the blocks.

113

Prop It Up

Skills & Concepts

✔ **Cooperating**

✔ **Identifying community workers**

✔ **Expressing creativity**

Materials

■ Blocks

■ Props and clothing used and worn by different community workers (hats, cooking utensils, badges, helmets, vests, and so on)

Variations

Rather than provide objects that are used by community workers, place objects in the block structures that might be used by circus performers, astronauts, or people in other fields of work.

Allow children to choose the props that will be placed in the block storage spaces. Ask them to look for objects that will fit inside the block structures as well as represent different kinds of work done by people in their community.

How To

1 Have children work together to build three block "storage spaces" to use with the different props. Tell children to leave an opening in each of these block structures so that you can place one prop inside each structure.

2 Ask children to close their eyes while you place a different prop in each of the storage spaces. Then tell them to open their eyes.

3 Have a child reach into the first block structure and carefully pull out the prop inside. Ask the child to dramatize an activity that would be performed by the community worker who would use this prop. For example, if a child pulls a rolling pin from one of the structures, he or she might act out a baker rolling dough with the rolling pin. Ask others in the group to try to identify the activity being dramatized.

4 Repeat the activity for the two remaining block structures. When finished, hide new objects inside each of the structures and play again.

Extending the Activity

Invite children to build replicas of their neighborhoods or community with blocks. They might include a fire station, car repair garage, grocery store, and so on. Encourage them to place objects, signs, and labels inside the structures to help identify them.

The Feature in the Square

Skills & Concepts

✔ **Developing gross motor skills**

✔ **Expressing creativity**

✔ **Role-playing**

Materials

■ Blocks

■ Costumes and props from the dramatic play area

How To

1. Work with children to build a large, open block square on the floor.

2. Introduce children to a game of "What Am I?" To do this, stand inside the block square, flap your arms, and make a "cawing" sound. Then ask: *What am I?* Encourage children to call out their responses.

3. Next, invite one child at a time to stand in the block square and imitate the movements or sounds of a person, animal, or thing. Remind children that they can use any of the available costumes or props to add to their dramatizations.

4. Challenge the other children to try to identify what the performer represents.

Variations

Place two parallel rows of blocks on the floor, spacing them about three feet apart. See how many different ways children can move along the area between the block rows. They might tiptoe, sway side to side, hop, and so on.

Play "Statue." Whisper to each child the name of something to dramatize, (perhaps a tree, a silly clown, or an airplane). Tell children that they will "freeze" in that role on your signal. Ask the other children to guess what each statue represents.

Extending the Activity

● Have children work together to create a series of roadways with blocks. When finished, have them use play vehicles to move up, down, and all around the roads. Ask: *What kind of vehicle are you? Where are you going? Who are your passengers?*

● Have children work together to create three large rectangles with blocks to represent clothes closets. Place several dress-up items from your dramatic play area into each of the "closets." Invite children to take the items from one of the closets and use them as props for a lively dramatization!

115

Plan, Build, and Pantomime

Skills & Concepts

✔ Cooperating
✔ Planning
✔ Expressing creativity

Materials

■ Blocks

How To

1 Tell children that both people and animals often use some sort of structures or buildings in their daily routines, whether they are at home, work, or play. Name a few examples, such as that doctors use a medical building, letter carriers use a post office, children use a school building, frogs use lily pads, and birds use nests. Invite children to name some additional examples.

2 Divide children into small groups. Invite each group to construct a block structure to represent a structure or building that an animal or a specific person, such as a doctor or letter carrier, might use. Encourage children to decide together what their structure will be and to plan how they will build it.

3 When the structures are completed, have the children in each group plan together how they will pantomime the person or animal that uses the kind of structure that they have built. Remind them to try to incorporate the structure in their performance, such as pretending to open and close the door to a building. Then invite one group at a time to perform its actions. Can the other groups identify what person or animal is being dramatized and what the structure represents?

Variation

Rather than constructing structures or buildings, invite children to build tools or machines with the blocks. When finished, have them pantomime how the tool or machine might be used. Ask the other children to try to identify the tool or machine being dramatized.

Extending the Activity

● Provide props such as dress-up clothes, briefcases, plastic dog bones, stuffed animals, and so on for children to use in their dramatizations.

● Invite children to describe a day in the life of the people or animals that might use their block structures. Write their dictation on chart paper. Then read the descriptions back to children. Later, display the descriptions near the appropriate block structures to inspire creativity in children's block-play activities.

Theater in the Round

Skills & Concepts

✔ Cooperating
✔ Planning
✔ Expressing creativity

Materials

- Blocks
- Dress-up clothes
- Booklets (made from stapled sheets of construction paper)
- White poster board (for signs)
- Markers, crayons, and pencils
- Index cards (for tickets)

Variations

Children might create a play based on their experiences during a recent field trip, a movie, or a story told to them by a family friend or relative.

Children can make costumes by decorating white sheets any way they like. Cut a hole for the head and arms and invite children to enjoy these self-designed costumes.

How To

1 Explain to children that they will create a theater in the block area. Then have them create a large block circle on the floor. Tell them that performances will take place within this large circle.

2 Discuss with children the type of performance that they might like to do, such as a dramatization of a favorite story or poem.

3 Invite children to use blocks to create props such as platforms, seats, low walls, and so on for their performance. Then have them choose dress-up clothes to use in their dramatization.

4 Work with children to make playbills from the construction-paper booklets. Have them include illustrations to depict what the performance is and who is in it. Also, help them make signs on posterboard and tickets on index cards.

5 On performance day, have children set up the signs, pass out tickets, and seat the audience. Then let the show begin!

Extending the Activity

● Invite the "audience" to review the performance with performers. What did the audience enjoy most about the performance? How did it make them feel? What other props would have helped with the performance? What other kinds of performances would they like to see in the future?

● Collect old theater tickets to share with children. Have them identify differences and similarities among the tickets, as well as specific letters, names, and numbers.

Blocks and Bows

Skills & Concepts

✔ **Understanding size relationships**

✔ **Describing**

✔ **Expressing creativity**

Materials

■ Blocks in various shapes and sizes

■ Gift bows

How To

1 Place the bows in the center. Ask children to select a block. Tell them that the block represents a gift. Then have them think of an imaginary object that they might be able to put in a box that's the same size as their selected block.

2 Have children put a gift bow on their pretend block gift.

3 Invite each child to exchange gifts with a classmate. When the classmate pretends to open the gift, have the gift-giver describe what the imaginary item inside is without naming the imaginary item. Challenge the classmate who received the gift to try to guess its identity.

Variations

Add a twist to the activity. Have children describe the imaginary surprise inside the gift that they "open." Remind them that what they describe should be able to fit into a package the size of their block gift. Can others guess what the surprise gift might be?

Encourage children to look around the classroom for an object that is about the size of their block gift. Have them describe that object for classmates to guess.

Extending the Activity

● Provide children with party favors and party snacks. Invite them to use the party items and their block gifts to role-play a birthday or holiday party.

● Give children boxes of different sizes. Ask them to put one block in each box, trying to match the size of the block as closely as possible to the size of the box.

ART CENTER

In these pages, you'll find ideas for introducing science, math, dramatic play, and literacy-building experiences in your art center. Use these activities to explore math and science concepts such as measurement and weight, inspire creative expression through music and drama, and encourage emerging literacy concepts such as letter and word recognition. There are many creative ways to extend children's learning and enjoyment when you use your art center to reinforce skills in curriculum areas from math to literacy. Just remember—more than painting can happen in your art center!

Art for All Seasons

Winter, spring, summer, and fall—art brings magic to them all!

Autumn Activities

Invite children to make fabulous confetti art creations with dried leaves! First, take them outdoors to collect a supply of dry leaves. Back in the classroom, help them draw large fall shapes, such as leaves, pumpkins, or apples, on a sheet of construction paper. Then have them crumble and glue the leaves onto the shapes. They might also add torn pieces of colorful tissue paper or construction paper.

Provide white construction paper, plastic forks, and paint in assorted fall colors. Invite children to dip a fork in paint and then rake it across the paper to create interesting designs. Or have them "rake-paint" fall-related pictures such as trees and pumpkins.

This "back-to-school" idea is packed with imagination! Each week during the first month of school, fill a backpack with different art materials. For instance, for the first week you might pack it with chalk, a spray bottle filled with water, construction paper, and oil pastels. Place the backpack in your art center. Then explain to children that they will use only the materials in the backpack—and their imagination—to create interesting pieces of artwork.

Winter Activities

Have children work in pairs to make handprints. Provide the partners with pencils, construction paper, scissors, and crayons. Ask each child to trace his or her partner's hands on a sheet of paper. Then help children cut out their handprints. Invite them to decorate their handprints with original designs and patterns to create a pair of gloves.

Ask children to describe their favorite snowy day activities, such as building snow people, making snow angels, digging tunnels, or building snow forts. If children have not had experiences in the snow, share picture books that feature snowy weather and different snow-related activities. Then invite them to create snowy day art using only white materials such as white poster board, white construction paper and tissue paper, cotton balls, and Styrofoam.

Provide children with a variety of craft materials such as construction paper, glitter, confetti, and ribbon. Invite them to use the materials to creatively design and make original winter holiday ornaments and decorations. They might also use pinecones, holly leaves, and pine needles to add a natural look to their creations.

120

Spring Activities

Introduce some colorful rainbow fun with this idea. Give children construction paper and ribbons or shredded paper strips in assorted colors. Have them draw a wide arch on their paper and divide it into several bands. Then invite them to glue a different color of ribbon or paper strip onto each band to create a beautiful rainbow. Display these colorful crafts on a bulletin board for the class and visitors to enjoy!

Cut sponges in a variety of shapes to represent flower petals and leaves. Have children use the shapes to sponge-print flowers on construction paper. Or have them print flowers on a length of bulletin board paper. They might also add other spring-related art, such as birds and butterflies. Display the flower-garden mural as a backdrop for a classroom center.

Spring is the perfect time for walking a pet! To encourage children's imaginations, invite them to decorate a long strip of paper to represent a leash. Then ask: *What kind of pet would you like to walk on your leash?* They might describe real or imaginary pets. After sharing, have children draw a picture of their pet, cut it out, attach it to the end of their leash, and then take it on an imaginary walk.

Summer Activities

Invite children to glue sand onto sheets of poster board to represent a beach. After the glue dries, have them shake off the excess sand and then use crayons or paint to create a beach scene on the sandy poster board. They might include a beach umbrella, beach ball, beach blanket, people, seagulls, seashells, sand castles, or any beach-related items of their choosing.

Have children work in pairs to trace their bare feet onto large sheets of paper. Then help them cut out their footprints. Invite children to use crayons, markers, and stamps and stamp pads to decorate their foot cutouts any way they like. Use the footprints to create an interesting border around a classroom bulletin board.

Invite children to tell about their experiences making sand sculptures. Then have them stir up a batch of sand dough. To begin, ask a small group to combine one cup flour, one cup sand, one cup water, and a half-cup of white glue. Have children mix the ingredients, adding more water as needed, until a textured dough forms. Invite them to use the dough to make "wet sand" sculptures and drawings. When finished, store the sand dough in a resealable plastic bag.

"On the Spot"

Art Center Celebrations

Hold a "When I Grow Up" celebration! Talk with children about the jobs they might like to have when they grow up. Then provide them with paper plates, crayons, and scissors. Invite children to use the materials to create masks that represent themselves in their desired job role. (Help them cut out eye and mouth holes from the paper plates.) When they complete their masks, have children glue a craft stick to the back. Later, ask children to take turns holding up their masks and pantomiming some of the duties they will perform when they begin their grown-up careers.

Plan a series of "spotlight parties" throughout the year. From time to time, shine a flashlight on a classroom object. Ask children to describe the object in as much detail as possible. Then place the object in the center of the art table. Invite children to draw, sculpt, or paint their own creative versions of the object. Later, encourage children to share—and celebrate—their artistic interpretations of the object with classmates.

Set aside special "Mystery Art" days. Decorate a large cardboard box with a wide variety of art materials such as ribbon, rickrack, stickers, glitter, paint, and cotton balls. For each mystery art day, fill the box with materials that have something in common. For instance, you might fill it with containers of play dough, sawdust dough, salt dough, and so on, making sure each type of dough has a different texture or consistency. Or you might fill it with shiny art materials such as glitter, tinsel, and foil wrapping paper. On the appointed day, invite a child to open the mystery box and distribute the surprise materials to classmates. Encourage children to share the materials as they explore and create with them.

Celebrate the changing seasons in your art center. First, cut out a large tree from a length of bulletin board paper. If possible, laminate the tree so that it can be reused throughout the year. Then, on the first day of each season, display the tree on a wall in or near the art area. Post a sign on the tree to welcome the new season. Next, discuss with children the activities that they look forward to doing in the new season. Have them draw pictures to represent their favorite activities. Then tape the drawings to the tree. Finally, ask children to describe their drawings while you write their dictation on paper. Attach each child's description to his or her drawing.

Recyclable Materials
for the Art Center

Here are some recyclable materials you'll want to have on hand to add interest and surprise to your art center.

Math in the Art Center

Materials	Possible Use
Sales flyers	for creating number collages
Old calendars	to create patterns by coloring the calendar blocks
Ribbon and yarn clippings	to decorate large outlines of numbers
Laundry detergent scoops	for measuring and comparing volumes of paint
Tags from purchased items	for sorting and creating patterns
Yogurt cups	to make paint-print patterns using cup rims and bottoms
Colored straws	for stringing, patterning, and comparing lengths
Styrofoam peanuts	to estimate and count the number needed to fill in shapes
Styrofoam trays	to decorate and use for sorting and counting
Pasta boxes with cellophane windows	to decorate, fill with manipulatives, and estimate quantity

Science in the Art Center

Materials	Possible Use
Paper scraps in assorted colors	for creating rainbow-related art
Bubble wrap	to shape and form into bubble-wrap insects
Plastic soda bottle lids	for filling homemade instruments to explore sound
Paper towel tubes	to make magnifiers, binoculars, telescopes, and microscopes
Candle stubs	to rub on paper and test resistance to water
Resealable plastic bags	to fill with different substances for sensory activities
Aluminum foil	to make impressions of different textures
Paper plates	for creating life-cycle mobiles
Toothpaste boxes	to decorate and store child-created mini-posters on hygiene
Plastic peanut butter jars	to decorate and use as planters

Literacy in the Art Center

Materials	Possible Use
Magazines and catalogs	for creating letter and word collages
Labels from canned and boxed foods	to create picture menus and recipes
Empty seed packets	to use as labels for painted garden scenes
Greeting cards	to cut out and use messages with own designs and drawings
Sponges cut into letter shapes	for paint-printing letters, words, and names
Cardboard	to use for V-shape stand-up messages or name cards
Styrofoam egg carton lids and trays	for etching impressions of letters and words
Shoe boxes	for making dioramas for favorite stories
Plastic forks	for "painting" letters
Gift boxes	for sorting items or pictures by beginning letter sounds

Dramatic Play in the Art Center

Materials	Possible Use
Fabric samples	to make items such as coasters and tablecloths
Price tags	to tape to sale items in "art store" play
Wrapping paper	to wrap surprise "gifts" for use in pretend parties
Plastic jug lids	to paint-print designs on handmade housekeeping items
Corrugated light bulb sleeves	to cut, shape, and decorate into jewelry for dress-up play
Netted potato and onion bags	to make textured impressions in play-dough foods
Cardboard pizza wheels	to decorate as food items for restaurant role-playing
Plastic cookie trays	for use as paint trays when role-playing artists
Facial tissue boxes	to decorate and use as personal treasure boxes
Soda bottles	to decorate and use for vases and other housekeeping items

And Try This!

Fast Food Cup Trays Cut fast food cup trays in half. Then cut out a circle from the bottom of each cup holder to create goggles. Have children paint the goggles, punch a hole in each side, and attach string ties. Then invite them to wear the goggles in their imaginary swimming activities.

Acorn Caps Invite children to glue one or more acorn caps onto a sheet of paper. Using the acorn caps as a starting point, have them create an entire picture around the caps. For example, an acorn cap might serve as a person's hat, a food bowl for an insect, or a "jewel" in a treasure chest.

Weighty Artwork

Skills & Concepts

✔ **Expressing creativity**

✔ **Estimating weight**

✔ **Comparing weight**

Materials

■ Boxes in various sizes and shapes (food boxes, shoe boxes, and so on)

■ Masking tape

■ Paints

■ Paintbrushes

■ Chart paper

■ Marker

■ Bathroom scale

How To

1️⃣ Place the collection of boxes in the art center. Explain that children will tape together boxes to create box sculptures. They can make abstract sculptures or sculptures that represent animals, vehicles, furniture, or any other object of their choice.

2️⃣ Ask children to select and tape boxes together to make their sculptures, providing help as needed.

3️⃣ Invite children to paint their sculptures. If desired, they might decorate their creations with additional craft items.

4️⃣ After children share their box sculpture with classmates, ask them to estimate how much it weighs. Write each child's estimate on chart paper beside his or her name. Then have children weigh their sculptures and compare the actual weight to their estimates.

Variation

Divide the boxes to create a set of boxes for every child in a group. Put a sticky note on all the boxes in a set and label each with the same number. Mix up the boxes. Have each child find all the boxes labeled with an assigned number and use them to build a sculpture.

Extending the Activity

● Challenge children to search the room for an object that might be equal in weight to their sculpture. Have them weigh the sculpture and the object. Do they weigh the same?

● Invite children to sequence the sculptures from heaviest to lightest by estimating the weight of each one. Have them weigh the sculptures to check their estimates.

A Code Full of Color

Skills & Concepts

✔ Recognizing numerals

✔ Matching colors

✔ Understanding codes

Materials

■ Poster board

■ Marker

■ Paint in ten different colors

■ Paintbrushes (one per paint color)

■ Easel paper (one sheet per child)

■ Crayons

How To

1 To prepare a color code chart, print the numerals 1–10 on the poster board. Paint a large color dot beside each numeral, using a different color for each dot.

2 Ask children to use crayons to write any of the numerals from 1–10 on a sheet of easel paper. They can use a few or all of the numerals and can arrange them on their paper in any way they choose. Encourage them to leave wide spaces between and around their numerals.

3 Use the prepared chart to explain the color code to children. Then tell them that they will paint a dot over each numeral on their page using the color of the dot beside the matching numeral on the chart (the crayon will repel the paint). When children finish, invite them to share their paintings with the group.

Variations

For a simpler version of this activity, ask children to write numerals on their paper with pencils. Then have them use crayons to color large dots next to the numerals.

Try using fabric swatches in the color code chart rather than paint. Provide matching fabric swatches for children to glue next to the numerals on their creations.

Extending the Activity

● Instead of color dots, use different kinds of lines and shapes beside the numerals. For instance, you might paint a vertical line, a horizontal line, a curvy line, a square, a triangle, and so on, each beside a different numeral. Have children refer to the new code and then paint the corresponding line or shape next to each numeral on their paper.

● Let children create their own numeral-color code charts. Have them exchange charts with classmates and then refer to the new charts to paint their papers.

Size It Up!

Skills & Concepts

✔ Matching shapes

✔ Comparing size

✔ Sequencing by size

Materials

- 9- by 12-inch white construction paper
- Items in different sizes and shapes that can be dipped in paint (buttons, sponge shapes, leaves, and so on)
- Finger paint
- Paint trays (one per paint color)
- Scissors

Variations

Invite children to use plastic shapes in different sizes to make paint prints. Then have them cut out and sort the prints by shape.

Have children paint-print plastic or rubber numbers in different sizes. Help them cut out each print. Invite them to sort the prints by size and then order them by number.

How To

1 Provide children with white construction paper, the collection of items, and paint trays containing shallow layers of paint. Have them choose an item, dip it into a paint tray, and then press it onto their paper to create a paint print of the item. Invite them to make a paint print for several different items.

2 After the paint dries, help children cut out their prints. Arrange the prints on a table. Then discuss with children the different shapes and sizes of their prints. Can they identify which item was used to make each print?

3 Distribute several prints of different sizes to each child in the group. Challenge the child to arrange the prints in order from smallest to largest.

Extending the Activity

● Invite children to choose several prints. Have them search the room to find items that are similar in size and shape to their prints.

● Create paint prints using several "mystery" objects around the classroom. Challenge children to search the room to find the objects that were used to make the prints.

Pick a Pattern

Skills & Concepts

✔ **Extending patterns**

✔ **Developing fine motor skills**

✔ **Identifying shapes**

Materials

■ Crayons, markers, paintbrushes, and chalk sticks (several of each)

■ 3-inch squares of tagboard (four per child)

Variations

Draw a series of shapes on a sheet of paper, using only the four shapes found on children's cards. Invite children to duplicate the pattern with their cards.

Have children use rubber stamps and stamp pads to make their cards. They might stamp the cards with shapes, coins, or numerals. Invite them to create repeating patterns with the cards.

How To

1 Line up a crayon, marker, paintbrush, and chalk stick on the table. Explain to children that you will make a pattern by adding more objects. Add another item of each kind to the line, putting the new items in the same order as the first ones.

2 Give a child one of each kind of item. Invite him or her to continue the pattern using the items. Ask other children to add items to repeat the pattern until all the items have been used.

3 Tell children that they will now create cards to use in making patterns. Help each child draw each of these shapes on a separate tagboard square: circle, square, rectangle, and triangle. (You might display these shapes for children to refer to as they draw.)

4 Place all the cards in the center of the table. Invite a child to start a pattern by using three or four cards with different shapes. Have a second child repeat the pattern. Encourage children to take turns repeating the pattern, using the available cards. When finished, invite children to "read" the pattern by naming the shapes in order from left to right.

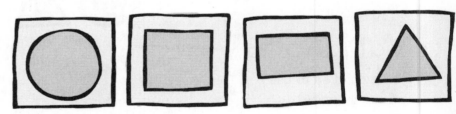

Extending the Activity

● Help children print numerals on their cards. Then have them use the cards to create repeating patterns of numerals.

● Have children pair up to play a pattern challenge game. To play, one child creates a pattern using the collection of cards. Then his or her partner duplicates the pattern. Encourage children to start with simple, short patterns. As they experience success in the game, have them create and duplicate more complicated patterns.

Colorful Creatures

Skills & Concepts

✔ **Expressing creativity**

✔ **Describing**

✔ **Sequencing by size**

Materials

■ Styrofoam balls in various sizes

■ Craft items including wiggle eyes, craft foam, fabric samples, cut paper towel tubes, pipe cleaners, pom-poms, ribbon, yarn, and so on

■ Scissors

■ Craft glue

How To

1 Invite children to tell about their favorite animals. Then ask: *What animal would you most like to have for a pet? Why? How would you care for your pet? What kinds of things would you do with it?*

2 Tell children that they will use craft materials to create their own pets. Their pets can be realistic or imaginary. Then invite children to choose a Styrofoam ball in the size of their choice. Have them decorate the ball to represent their unique and special pet.

3 Invite children to name their pets. Then have them show their pet to classmates as they describe its habits, food preferences, favorite activities, and other information.

4 After sharing, have children sequence their pets from smallest to largest. Ask: *Which pet is the smallest? The largest? Which ones are medium-sized?*

Variation

Have children create original characters rather than pets. Encourage them to name and describe their characters before sequencing them from smallest to largest.

Extending the Activity

● Provide boxes in assorted sizes for children to decorate and use as beds for their pets. Invite children to "tuck" their pets into the beds and then arrange the beds from smallest to largest.

● Encourage children to compare the sizes of details on their decorated pets. Ask: *What is the smallest part of your pet? The largest? The longest? The shortest?* They might also compare the size of features on their pets to similar features on classmates' pets.

Step Up to Measure Up

Skills & Concepts

✔ **Expressing creativity**

✔ **Estimating height**

✔ **Comparing height**

Materials

■ Measuring tape

■ Five-foot lengths of bulletin board paper, cut into 6-inch wide strips (one strip per child)

■ Pencil

■ Collage materials including ribbon, yarn, tissue paper, string, fabric scraps, stickers, and so on

■ Scissors

■ Glue

How To

1 Use the measuring tape to find each child's height. Write the child's name and height on the back of a strip of bulletin board paper. Then cut the strip to that child's height.

2 Invite children to use the collage materials to decorate their paper strips. Encourage them to create interesting patterns and designs on their strips, being as creative and original as possible.

3 Display children's decorated paper strips on a classroom wall. Make sure the bottom of each strip meets the floor.

4 Point to one strip at a time. Challenge children to try to guess who the strip belongs to. To check their guesses, ask each child who was named as the possible creator to stand beside the paper strip. Does his or her height match the height of the strip? If more than one child measures the same height, ask the owner of the strip to step forward.

Variations

Have children cut and decorate paper strips equal to the length of their arms or legs.

Instead of using collage materials, invite children to decorate their paper strips by painting designs and patterns along the length of their strips.

Extending the Activity

What objects in the classroom or around the school might be the same height as children? Invite children to measure their decorated strips against different objects to determine if they are shorter, taller, or about the same size as the objects!

It's in the Clouds!

Skills & Concepts

✔ **Observing**

✔ **Expressing creativity**

✔ **Describing**

Materials

■ 9- by 12- inch and 12- by 18- inch white construction paper (one of each size per child)

■ 9- by 12- inch sheets of cardboard (one per child)

■ Clothespins

■ Crayons

■ Scissors

■ Glue

■ Watercolors

■ Paintbrushes

How To

1 Take children outdoors on a cloudy day. Take along an art bag filled with 9- by 12- inch sheets of white construction paper, cardboard, clothespins, and crayons.

2 Find a cozy place for children to settle down. Then have them look at the sky. What do they see? Are there any shapes in the clouds? Do any of the clouds look alike? Different? Invite children to share their observations with the group.

3 Pass out a piece of cardboard and sheet of 9- by 12-inch white construction paper to each child. Help the child attach the paper to the cardboard with a clothespin, creating a clipboard for the paper. Then have the child use crayons to draw a cloud formation on his or her paper. The cloud might resemble the shape of an object or it might just be a big, puffy cloud shape. While at work, encourage children to describe their drawings.

4 Back in the classroom, invite children to paint their own interpretations of the sky on a sheet of 12- by 18-inch white construction paper. Then have them cut out and glue their cloud drawings onto their paintings. After the paint dries, encourage children to share and describe their creations with the class.

Variation

Share a few books about the night sky with children. Have them sketch a picture of what they might see if they were looking at a night sky.

Extending the Activity

Show children pictures of different types of weather, including cloudy, sunny, stormy, and wintry conditions. Invite them to paint pictures of these different weather conditions.

Fabulous Floaters!

Skills & Concepts

✔ **Predicting buoyancy**

✔ **Exploring buoyancy**

✔ **Classifying**

Materials

■ Styrofoam items (cups, plates, trays, packing peanuts, blocks, and so on)

■ Cardboard

■ Aluminum foil

■ Plastic wrap

■ Assorted art materials (paper and fabric scraps, craft foam, craft sticks, and so on)

■ Pipe cleaners, yarn, and twist ties

■ Water table (or large container of water)

How To

1 Show children the collection of materials. Ask: *Which items float? Which sink?* Have them place each item in water to test their predictions. Then have them sort the materials according to whether they float or sink.

2 Have children examine the items that sink. Can any of these materials be formed into a shape that floats? Invite them to experiment to discover whether or not the shape of a material makes a difference. (For example, a wrinkled piece of foil sinks, but when shaped into a boat, the foil floats.)

3 Ask children to name and describe different kinds of flotation devices. They might mention rafts, swim rings, animal-shaped swim tubes, and so on.

4 Invite children to create mini flotation devices from the art materials provided. Encourage them to use a material that floats for the foundation of their creations. They can attach decorative materials to their flotation devices with pipe cleaners, yarn, or twist ties.

Variation

Invite children to create boats with the provided materials, rather than flotation devices. Have them test their boats in the water to discover whether they float or sink.

Extending the Activity
Place a variety of art materials in a box. Have children predict whether each item will sink or float when placed in water. Then have them test their predictions. Write each item on a chart under the corresponding heading "Sink" or "Float." Later, discuss the similarities and differences between the items under both headings.

Framed by Nature's Bounty

Skills & Concepts

✔ **Exploring nature**

✔ **Observing nature**

✔ **Expressing creativity**

Materials

■ Paper bags
   (one per child)

■ Nature items (collected
   by children)

■ 9- by 12-inch white
   construction paper
   (one sheet per child)

■ Watercolors

■ 12- by 15-inch sheets
   of colored construction
   paper (one per child)

■ Glue

How To

1 Give children paper bags to take on a nature walk. Invite them to collect pinecones, tree bark, leaves, small stones, and other nature items. While outdoors, encourage them to notice the sights all around them. Back in classroom, have them set the nature items aside for later use.

2 Pass out the watercolors and 9- by 12- inch sheets of white construction paper. Have children paint a picture of a natural sight they observed on their walk. They might paint a simple picture of trees and the sky, or a more detailed picture of an insect on a twig. Encourage them to keep the focus of their paintings on nature, rather than people, buildings, vehicles, or other things.

3 To create a "frame," help children glue their painting to the center of a 12- by 15-inch sheet of construction paper.

4 Invite children to use the nature items they collected earlier to decorate their frames.

Variations

Invite children to create collages with their nature items and then decorate their frames with painted patterns and designs.

"Pose" one or more nature items on a table. Have children paint the nature still-life and then decorate the frame around the painting with real nature items.

Extending the Activity

● Invite children to describe their paintings and the nature items on the frame. Ask questions such as: *What is the item? Does it come from a living or nonliving source? How does it feel?*

● After a few weeks, return to the path of your nature walk. Have children look for the same kind of items they used on their frames. Ask: *Do the items on the frames look different from the fresh nature items? If so, how are they different? Why are they different?*

It's All in the Balance

Skills & Concepts

✔ **Exploring attributes**

✔ **Exploring balance**

✔ **Comparing weights**

Materials

■ Paper lunch bags

■ Rocks in different sizes and shapes

■ Newspaper

■ Poster paints

■ Paintbrushes

■ Balance

How To

1 Give children paper bags to take on an outdoor rock hunt. Encourage them to collect rocks in many different sizes. Tell them that all the rocks they collect should fit inside their bag.

2 Back in the classroom, have children spread out their rocks on a sheet of newspaper. To help them share their findings, ask children to show the group specific rocks, such as the smallest, largest, roughest, the two most similar or different rocks, and so on.

3 Invite children to paint a few of their rocks in any way they desire. For example, they might paint one a solid color, another with polka-dots, and another with a bold pattern. Or they might paint their rocks to resemble insects, animals, or people.

4 After the paint dries, have children experiment with balancing their rocks on the balance. Can they put an equal number of rocks on each side to balance the scale? If so, are all the rocks the same size? Why might one rock weigh more than several rocks together? Encourage children to answer these and similar questions as well as to share their discoveries about weight and balance.

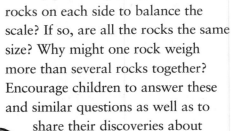

Variations

Invite children to create animals, vehicles, or other objects with their rocks. Have them experiment with balancing their creations on the balance.

Place two painted rocks in separate boxes and close the lids. Invite children to predict which box contains the heavier rock. Have them use the balance to test their predictions.

Extending the Activity

● Ask children to search for a classroom object that they predict weighs about the same as one of their painted rocks. Have them place the rock and the object on the balance to test their prediction.

● Invite children to work in pairs. Ask each child to choose a rock from his or her collection that is about the same size as one chosen by his or her partner. Have children place the rocks on the balance to discover whether or not they weigh the same.

Lovely Letter Trees

Skills & Concepts

✔ **Recognizing letters**

✔ **Developing fine motor skills**

✔ **Comparing printed letters**

Materials

■ 12- by 18-inch construction paper (one sheet per child)

■ Marker

■ Old magazines

■ Scissors

■ Glue

How To

1 Give each child a sheet of construction paper. Ask the child to draw a large tree on the paper. Then write the first letter of the child's name on the tree using large, bold print. You also might write the child's name in small print at the bottom of the tree.

2 Have children search magazines to find letters that match the first letter of their name. Help them cut out the letters. Then have them glue the letters onto their tree.

3 When finished, invite children to share their letter trees with the group. Discuss with them how the same letter can have many different looks. Then have them point out the similarities and differences between the sizes, shapes, typefaces, and other characteristics of the letters on their trees.

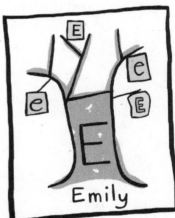

Variations

Invite children to search magazines to find words that begin with the first letter of their names. Have them cut out and glue the words onto their trees.

Challenge children to cut out pictures of things that begin with the same sound as the first letter of their names. After they glue the pictures to their trees, use the trees to reinforce initial letter sounds.

Extending the Activity

● Use the letter trees to inspire children to make up a story about the "Forest of Letter Trees." Write their dictated story on chart paper. Then invite children to create illustrations for the story.

● Place each child's letter tree near a sheet of chart paper taped to the floor. Invite the child to refer to the letter on the tree as he or she draws or paints the same letter on the paper.

Read that Rebus!

Skills & Concepts

✔ **Developing stories**

✔ **Expressing creativity**

✔ **Reading**

Materials

■ Rebus stories

■ Chart paper

■ Marker

■ Crayons

Once there was a giant 🐟 *.*

How To

1 Share a rebus story with children. Then tell them they will help create a rebus story. As children watch, print the beginning of a story on a sheet of chart paper. You might write a sentence starter similar to "Once there was a giant...."

2 Read the sentence starter to children. Then invite a child to draw a picture next to the sentence starter to complete the sentence. Ask the child to "read" the sentence to classmates, filling in the name of the picture when he or she comes to it. For example, if the child drew a fish at the end of the sentence starter, he or she will read "Once there was a giant fish."

3 Write additional sentence starters or incomplete sentences that can be connected to tell a story. Be sure to leave space for children to draw a picture in the missing part of each sentence. Each time you add a sentence, invite a child to draw a picture to complete the sentence and then "read" the sentence aloud.

4 When finished, invite children to read along as you read the rebus story aloud.

Variations

Invite children to use stickers or magazine cutouts in their rebus story. When completed, invite children to "read" their stories to the class.

Read a rebus poem to children. Then have them work together to create a rebus poem to share with the class.

Extending the Activity

● Make a word list for the pictures that children drew in their rebus story. Display the list next to the story. As children "read," have them find the word for each picture.

● Prepare a rebus story frame by using incomplete sentences and leaving space for children to add pictures. Laminate the story frame. Invite children to use wipe-off markers to add their drawings. After they "read" the story, they can erase the pictures and add different ones to create a new story!

What's in a Label?

Skills & Concepts

✔ **Identifying letters**

✔ **Recognizing words**

✔ **Reading pictures**

Materials

■ Assorted labels from jars, cans, postal packages, food boxes, plastic containers, and so on

■ 12- by 18-inch white construction paper (one sheet per child)

■ Markers

■ Glue

Variations

Have children sort the labels by size, shape, or type (such as food labels, mail labels, beverage labels, and so on). If desired, have them glue labels from only one group onto their jars.

Invite children to sort the labels into three groups: those with words only, those with pictures only, and those with both pictures and words. When finished, they can glue the labels of their choice onto their jars.

How To

1 Place the collection of labels in the center of a table. Invite children to explore the labels. Ask: *Do you see any letters that you know? Any words? Do any of the labels have words with pictures? Can you read the words?* Ask children to tell what kinds of information they might find on labels.

2 For each child, draw a large jar on a sheet of construction paper. Tell children that they will choose labels to glue onto their jars. As they work, have them continue to point out letters and words that they recognize. Ask them to share what they know about the sounds made by letters they come across. Have children tell where specific letters might be found, such as the first letter in their names. Also encourage them to "read" the pictures.

3 When finished, display children's label collages on a classroom wall or bulletin board.

Extending the Activity

● Encourage children to create their own labels! They might design labels for jars of spaghetti sauce, jelly, or pickles. Help children, as needed, to write letters and words onto their labels.

● Pair up children. Ask one child to point out a letter or word on his or her collage. Have the child's partner search his or her own collage for a matching letter or word.

Super-Sized Stamps

Skills & Concepts

✔ **Expressing creativity**
✔ **Developing fine motor skills**
✔ **Writing**

Materials

- 5-inch squares of white paper (one per child)
- Used postage stamps featuring a variety of images
- Markers
- Crayons
- Scissors
- 12- by 18-inch white construction paper (one sheet per child)
- Glue

Variations

For smaller stamps, have children decorate plain index cards. For larger stamps, they can decorate 9- by 12-inch sheets of construction paper and then glue them onto a sheet of chart paper turned lengthwise.

Ask children to create stamps related to a theme, such as things that symbolize our country.

How To

1 Invite children to explore the collection of stamps. Talk about the different images on the stamps. Then let each child tell which stamp is his or her favorite and why.

2 Tell children that they will design their own giant stamps! Show them a 5-inch paper square. Tell them that this will be the size of their stamps.

3 Encourage children to mentally plan how they want their stamps to look. Then pass out the squares of white paper. Invite children to use markers or crayons to create their "stamps."

4 Ask children to glue their giant stamps in the upper right corner of a giant "envelope" (a large sheet of construction paper). Help them address their envelopes to a classmate at the school address (you might assign each child the name of a child in another group). Then help them write their own name in the upper left corner.

5 Collect the envelopes. Invite children to take turns "reading" the addresses and delivering the "mail" to classmates. As they receive mail, encourage children to check the return address to discover who sent it.

Mary Jones

John Smith
Elm Street School

Extending the Activity

● Invite children to "write" a letter to send home to a family member or caregiver. Help them address their envelopes. Then have them affix a stamp and drop the letter into a mailbox.

● Bring in junk mail. Have children compare the envelopes to find identical words and uppercase and lowercase letters on them.

Unique Invitations

Skills & Concepts

✔ Planning

✔ Writing

✔ Expressing creativity

Materials

■ Sheets of white copy paper (one per child)

■ Markers

■ Chart paper

■ Samples of different kinds of invitations (optional)

■ Crayons

■ Healthy party treats

How To

1 Decide on a date and time for a class party. Then fold a sheet of paper in half to create an invitation. On the inside write "It's a Party!" Also include "Place," "Date," and "Time," and a blank line next to each word. Copy a class supply of the invitation.

2 Write the text from the invitation on chart paper. Fill in the blanks with the place, date, and time of the party.

3 Tell children that they will throw an art party! To prepare, they will make invitations for their choice of toy friends in the classroom, such as stuffed animals, dolls, and plastic figures.

4 After children decide (secretly) which toy friend to invite, help them write the place, date, and time on a copy of the invitation, referring to the invitation on the chart paper as needed. Then have them fold and decorate their cards, using the art materials of their choice.

5 On the morning of the party, have children place their invitations next to their chosen guests. Just before the party, send volunteers to gather the guests. After children enjoy their snacks—with their guests seated beside them—have them create a special work of art to celebrate...art!

Variation

Have small groups of children make invitations for each other. On the appointed day, children can hand out their invitations, gather to enjoy treats with each other, and then work together to create a piece of art.

Extending the Activity

● Help small groups create posters to announce the party information. Encourage children to work together to plan how the poster will look, as well as to create it.

● Ask children to create invitations for a class celebration to send home. Help them write the information on the inside of their invitations. Then have them decorate the front of their invitations with the craft materials of their choice.

Rackets, Nets, and More!

Skills & Concepts

✔ Planning
✔ Developing fine motor skills
✔ Role-playing

Materials

- Pictures of people playing different sports (tennis, golf, soccer, and so on)
- Assorted recyclable items (nylon net produce bags, clean laundry scoops, paper towel tubes, and so on)
- Scissors
- Glue
- Masking tape

How To

1 Show children the pictures of people playing different sports. Talk about the equipment used for each sport. Invite children to tell about their own sports-playing experiences and the related equipment.

2 Place the recyclable items on the table. Explain that children can use any of the provided materials, as well as any materials in the art center, to create a piece of sports equipment. Invite them to explore the materials as they decide what to make. Encourage children to mentally plan how they will make their pieces of equipment before beginning to construct them.

3 When ready, invite children to "build" their equipment. They might make golf clubs with laundry scoops and wrapping paper tubes, or tennis and badminton rackets with net produce bags, cardboard, and wide craft sticks. Encourage children to be creative!

4 When finished, invite children to take turns pretending they are playing the sport represented by their equipment. Have them use their equipment as props in their role-playing. Challenge classmates to guess the sport and equipment being used in each performance.

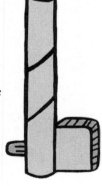

Variation

Invite children to role-play their chosen sport without props. Then have them add their homemade equipment to their performance. Which performance makes guessing the sport easier?

Extending the Activity

● Print on chart paper the name of each sport represented by children's homemade equipment. Then place all the equipment together. Read the name of one sport at a time. Have children try to match the appropriate equipment to that sport.

● Take children outdoors. Invite them to use soft balls and rackets of different sizes to devise their own games. Have them make up rules for the game and then invite other classmates to play.

Shape It, Imitate It

Skills & Concepts

✔ Exploring figures

✔ Forming shapes

✔ Developing fine motor skills

Materials

■ Half-sheets of 9- by 12-inch construction paper

■ 8-inch lengths of yarn

■ Glue

How To

1 Glue a length of yarn in a straight line on a sheet of paper. Have children look at the line and describe it. They might describe is as a straight line, a line that goes up and down, or a long (or tall) line. Then invite children to duplicate the yarn line using their bodies.

2 Give children a sheet of paper and a length of yarn. Have them glue their yarn onto the paper in any shape or form that they desire. They might glue the yarn to form a circle, a zigzag line, or a V shape.

3 Invite one child at a time to show the group his or her paper. Have the group try to duplicate the yarn figure with their bodies.

4 After the activity, invite children to glue more yarn designs to their papers to create interesting works of art.

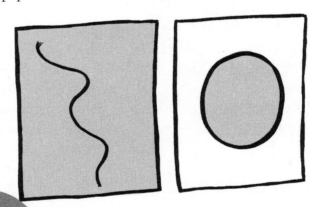

Variations

Rather than yarn, provide children with lengths of ribbon or thin rope. Encourage them to be creative in making their shapes on paper.

Spread out the yarn figures on the floor. Have children move from one figure to another, stopping at each one to duplicate it with their bodies.

Extending the Activity

● After children duplicate the yarn figures with their bodies, have them draw the figures on a separate sheet of paper. Encourage them to try to make their drawings as close as possible in form and size to the original figures.

● Challenge children to work together to create one large picture from all of their yarn designs. Have them plan how they will assemble the pages and where and how they will add more yarn to create the planned picture.

Music Magic

Skills & Concepts

✔ **Expressing creativity**

✔ **Exploring sound**

✔ **Inventing rhythms**

Materials

■ Cardboard and plastic containers in assorted sizes and shapes (pasta boxes, soap boxes, oatmeal canisters, butter tubs, and so on)

■ Paper towel tubes

■ Bubble wrap

■ Sandpaper

■ Uncooked rice

■ Tape

■ Regular and wide craft sticks

■ Scissors

Variations

Inspire children with some background music as they explore the sound-making materials and create their instruments.

Display pictures of different kinds of instruments. Invite children to refer to the pictures as they plan and create their own instruments.

How To

1 Show children the collection of materials. Ask them to share ideas about how some of the materials might be used to make instruments. For example, they might suggest gluing sandpaper onto two soap boxes to make sand blocks, or tapping a stick on a lidded butter tub to make a drum, or filling a yogurt cup with rice to make a maraca. (Be sure to securely tape closed any instruments that contain rice.)

2 Invite children to explore sounds that can be made by combining two or more of the provided materials. When children discover materials that work together to create a sound they like, have them use the materials to make an instrument. They might create a familiar instrument or a new and unique creation!

3 After making their instruments, invite children to decorate their creations with any available art materials in the art center.

4 When finished, invite children to hold a parade. Have them march around the room or an outdoor play space while they play their homemade instruments. Encourage children to take turns inventing rhythms for classmates to echo. Also have them compare and contrast the different sounds made by the different instruments.

Extending the Activity

● Have children explore the sounds made by different rhythm band instruments in the classroom. Are the sounds made by their homemade instruments similar to any of the class instruments?

● Play some simple marching music. Have children try to replicate the sounds and rhythms of the music with their homemade instruments.

Stuck Like Glue!

Skills & Concepts

✔ **Role-playing**

✔ **Creating patterns**

✔ **Cooperating**

Materials

■ Glue stick

■ Scraps of paper

Variations

To add interest, play some lively music as children role-play sticking themselves together.

Tape a length of bulletin board paper to the wall. Invite children to be creative in using the paper in their role-playing. For example, the "glue stick" might attach one "paper scrap" to the large paper at the knee, another at the head, and another at the elbow.

How To

1 Show children a glue stick. Ask them to tell how and why a glue stick is used.

2 Use the glue stick to glue together the edges of two different colors of scrap paper. Then add a third paper scrap of a different color. Invite each child to glue a paper scrap to the strip to extend the color pattern.

3 Tell children that they will pretend to be glue sticks and paper scraps. By working together, they will create a color pattern of paper scraps, much like the one they just created. Then appoint one child to be the glue stick and the others to be scrap paper.

4 To role-play, the glue stick "glues" together two or three paper scraps to create a color pattern (based on the color of children's clothing). The glue stick continues sticking paper scraps together to repeat the pattern as many times as possible.

5 Reassign roles and repeat the activity until every child has had a turn to be the glue stick.

Extending the Activity

● Instead of glue and scraps of paper, have children use pipe cleaners. Simply have them hook the ends of the pipe cleaners to connect them together. After making a pipe-cleaner chain, invite children to take the role of pipe cleaners and assemble themselves into a human pipe-cleaner chain.

● Invite children to explore and role-play other art materials in the art center. For instance, they might become unraveled balls of yarn, squeezed sponges, dipped paint brushes, or inked rubber stamps!

Dramatic Play Masterpieces

Skills & Concepts

✔ **Expressing creativity**

✔ **Cooperating**

✔ **Describing**

Materials

■ Poster board

■ Poster paints

■ Paintbrushes

■ Construction paper strips in assorted colors

■ Glue

Variations

Instead of poster paint, invite children to use tempera paint, oil pastels, or watercolors to create their masterpieces.

Invite children to create masterpiece play-dough sculptures to use in their role-playing activities. Encourage them to plan and sculpt pieces that might be used to enhance any role-playing theme.

How To

1 Discuss with children the different theme-related activities they enjoy in the dramatic play area. What are their favorite themes? Housekeeping? Restaurant? Department store? Hospital? After sharing, tell them that they will paint pictures to use in their thematic role-playing activities.

2 Have two or three children work together. Ask children to decide what theme they want to create a painting for and what to include in their painting. When ready, give groups a poster board and have them set to work on their creations. As children work, encourage them to describe their paintings and the kinds of role-playing activities that might take place around their artwork.

3 When finished, help children glue construction paper strips around the edges of their painting to create a frame. Invite them to display their painting and then role-play activities related to the theme represented by their artwork.

Extending the Activity

● Spread out the paintings on a table. Invite children to carefully examine them to decide which paintings seem most appropriate for a specific role-playing theme, such as a supermarket, birthday party, or magic show theme. Have them display those paintings when they role-play activities for the selected theme.

● Encourage children to create other types of props to enhance their role-playing activities. For example, they might create a backdrop from an old sheet, a treasure chest from a large box, or hats from newspaper.